Diane Olson

May 1996

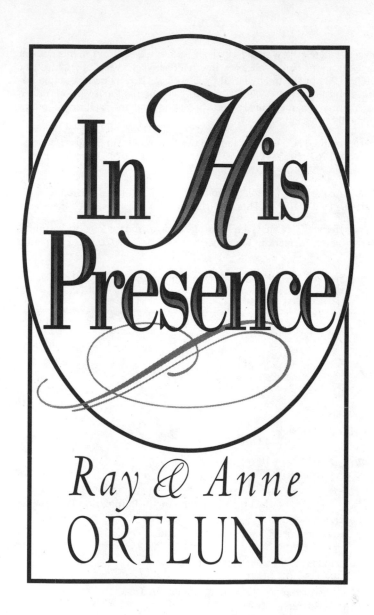

In His Presence

Ray & Anne ORTLUND

HARVEST HOUSE
PUBLISHERS
Eugene, Oregon 97402

IN HIS PRESENCE

Copyright ©1995 by Harvest House Publishers
Eugene, Oregon 97402

Library of Congress Cataloging-in-Publication Data
Ortlund, Raymond C.
    In his presence / Ray and Anne Ortlund.
        p.   cm.
    Includes bibliographical references.
    ISBN 1-56507-282-0
    1. Christian life.   I. Ortlund, Anne.   II. Title.
    BV4501.2.07264   1995
    248—dc20   95-7291
                                                CIP

Printed in the United States of America.

To Immanuel,
"God with us"

Contents

Part Four
The Experience of His Presence

Part Five
A One-Week Experiment

In His Presence

There are some truths that
are too big to enter by the
narrow slit of reason.
—PLATO

The Invitation
to
His Presence

Who is he who will devote
himself to be close to me?
—JEREMIAH 30:21

1

The Response of the Two of Us, and Many Others

We two Ortlunds were sprawled out on our stomachs on the beach. It was August, and it was the middle year of our 20 years of pastoring Lake Avenue Congregational Church in Pasadena, California. We were vacationing, seeking to recover from the deep, though blessed, fatigue of pastoring.

The sun was warm, the sand was warm. We lay on beach towels, propping up our heads as we read to each other from Brother Lawrence's *The Practice of the Presence of God*. And we said to each other,

> Attention to God was to be not just a slot of time every day, but all day long, every day. His presence was to permeate everything. We would commit ourselves to do everything for the love of God, in simple rest and without fear.
>
> We would seek to live as if absolutely nothing mattered except loving God, pleasing God, trusting God. . . .
>
> The psalmists had sung to God, and so would we,
> "I am always with you; you hold me by my right hand" (PSALM 73:23).

3

"My heart says of you, 'Seek his face!' Your face, Lord, I will seek" (PSALM 27:8).

"I have set the Lord always before me. Because he is at my right hand, I will not be shaken" (PSALM 16:8).

We would never be the same again.

We taught this "Priority One" truth (of fresh love for God), along with "Priority Two" (fresh love for fellow believers) and "Priority Three" (fresh love for the world) to our congregation that fall, and slow-burn revival began which lasted for years.[1] In February we taught it to the students of Wheaton College, and God gave a week of revival. We taught it soon in Colombia, in Peru, at Taylor University, in Ecuador. . . . In each place revival came.

Out of truths which God taught us in those few months came all of our book-writing and conference speaking and a together-life permanently reshaped.

But we shouldn't have written a book on living in His presence until now. God knew that other books had to come first, while we slowly absorbed His presence into our lives and studied it and experienced it and watched it in others.

In the first few months we held each other accountable to establish the new habit.

Anne to Ray, as he grumpily shaved one morning:
    "Ray, are you practicing the Presence?"

Ray: "Of course not! What do you think!" We laughed. . . .

Ray: Set his wristwatch alarm every 15 minutes to call him back to thoughts of God. . . .

Anne: Put a paper on the floor beside her bed with "JESUS" written on it, to bring her, first thing in the morning, to the worship of Him. . . .

Ray: Put sticky-papers on his desk, shaving mirror, car dashboard, which said "PTP" ("Practice the Presence"). . . .

At first, excited as we were, we didn't understand exactly how everything else we knew fit with His presence. Now, years later, we see that His presence has permeated everything else we know.

Is the real presence of God in a human life available? Is it obtainable? Is it a central truth of Christianity, worth spending your time exploring? Is it possible for you, reading this book? Yes, it truly is!

Children who know Jesus accept this truth simply. "Where is Jesus?" you ask them, and they answer, "He's in my heart." But to grow up aware of and enjoying God's presence—most Christians seem to know little about this, nor do they seek it.

Oh, listen—the most important thing one person (or couple) can do for another is to bring him (or her) into the presence of God, and leave him there! We want to do that in this book.

Living in His presence is the secret to living. We're writing these words because we're beginning to live it—

feebly, perhaps, but the little we know about consciously being moment by moment in the presence of the Lord is sweeter, deeper, grander, happier, more cleansing, more motivating, more restful, more energizing, more purposeful, more exhilarating than anything else we know.

Frank Laubach, late missionary to the Philippines, knew this secret. He wrote in his diary:

> August 21, 1930. I shall be forty-six in two weeks. . . . As we grow older all our paths diverge, and in all the world I suppose I could find nobody who could wholly understand me except God—and neither can you!
>
> Oh, God, what a new nearness this brings for Thee and me, to realize that Thou alone canst understand me, for Thou alone knowest all! Thou art all the way inside with me—here.[2]

We two are feeling that more and more. When we quarrel because we don't understand each other, there is One to whom we can go; and nearness to Him brings us back again to nearness to each other.

Bernard of Clairvaux, thirteenth century, knew His presence. He wrote:

> Jesus, the very thought of Thee
>   With sweetness fill my breast;
> But sweeter far Thy face to see
>   And in Thy presence rest.[3]

In the first few years of practicing His presence we thought that thinking much *about* Him, during the course of a day, was all we could hope for—and it was wonderful, and no doubt kept us out of a lot of trouble! But even writing this book has brought us more face-to-face with Him, and it is both restful and glorious.

David Hazard knows the secret. He wrote in 1992:

> If just once you catch sight of the love of God, you will know the joy of living in His presence. And a single day in God's presence, as the psalmist sings, is better than gold.[4]

We must tell you that we didn't understand the intimate connection between His love and His presence until this year, working on this book. The overall truth of Chapters 2 and 3 is thrillingly new to us.

W. Y. Fullerton knew God's presence. He wrote in 1916:

> A saint whose name is fragrant over the world was once asked to put in a sentence what had brought such joy and victory into his own life, and he answered in the words of the psalmist, "I have set the Lord always before me."
>
> That is the secret of everything, that is the true source of comfort, that is the solution of every spiritual difficulty. In the world you can never learn anything for this mortal life beyond that, and nowhere on earth can you need more.[5]

How often we two counsel Christians who are worried, nervous, anxious, and thrashing around! They know Christ as their Savior, but to them He's 'way up there in heaven, and what's omnipresent is their problem. What a pity; what a waste!

Francis of Assisi knew the presence of God. In about A.D. 1225 he wrote:

> Let us make a home within our soul, a dwelling place for the Lord God Almighty—Father, Son and Holy Spirit.[6]

He in us, and we in Him. The two of us are beginning to learn ACTS 17:28 in our personal experience: "In him we live and move and have our being."

Thomas Kelly knew the presence. Around 1940 he wrote:

> Deep within us all there is an amazing inner sanctuary of the soul, a holy place, a Divine Center, a Speaking Voice, to which we may continuously return. . . . It is the Shekinah of the soul, the Presence in the midst.[7]

People here and there have always found the presence of God. Adam and Eve walked with Him in the cool of the day. Abraham, Isaac, and Jacob built altars to Him. Moses and Joshua met Him in a tent. David "sat before the Lord" (2 SAMUEL 7:18). Ezekiel met Him by a river; Daniel, on his knees; the apostle John, simply "in the Spirit."

You are no stranger to God. He planned for you, believer, from before the foundation of the world, and His plan was *to be with you*. And He invites you to realize it, to come into a continual awareness of His presence and be revolutionized by it.

This is the secret to life.

Wrote the psalmist David:

> *You have made known to me the path of life;*
> *   you will fill me with joy in your presence,*
> *   with eternal pleasures at your right hand*
>   (PSALM 16:11).

Come with us. You discover it too.

2

The Love of God

There is a truth which, if you believe it, will bring you to the secret, and to joy beyond expressing. The truth is this: *God loves you.*

You sang it when you were little: "Jesus loves me, this I know, for the Bible tells me so."

But as you grew older (if you're typical) you didn't pursue what His love is all about, and you've spent your years in hopes and disappointments, wonderings and fears, ups and downs.

> *The one who fears is not made perfect in love*
> (1 JOHN 4:18).

God wants you to be made perfect in love. We're not talking primarily about your love for Him; anybody's love for God would be a shaky foundation indeed to build upon. We're talking about *God's love for you:* purer, stronger, larger, more persevering than you've probably realized.

> *Whoever is wise, let him . . . consider the great love*
> *of the Lord* (PSALM 107:43).

Understanding God's love for you is the foundation—and the motivation—for practicing His presence. Who wants to draw near to someone who he only thinks of as far away, judgmental, awesome, and austere? That's how Christians in their own human wisdom think of God, and they're not naturally drawn to that! So although they expect to go someday to heaven, they assume that for now they'll just have to muddle along mostly on their own.

God's desire is for you to come close to Him.

That's why He yearns for you to—

> grasp how wide and long and high and deep is the love of Christ, and to know this love that surpasses knowledge—that you may be filled to the measure of all the fullness of God (EPHESIANS 3:18,19).

Our son-in-law Walt Harrah has written a song you may be singing at your church:

> Think about His love; think about His goodness;
> Think about His grace that's brought us through . . .

Come along with the two of us and think about it.

God wants you to see Him as loving, tender, kind, and good; then you'll be drawn to live in His presence. Christ came to earth to show you how good God the Father is and how much He loves you (JOHN 14:21). The Holy Spirit has been given to you to teach you how good your Father is and how much He loves you (ROMANS 5:5).

*God's great requirement of you is that you believe and ac-
cept His love for you!* Pursue this now more deeply, more
freshly, than you ever have before.

It's because God loves you—personally—so much that
He planned for your salvation:

> *God so loved the world that he gave his one and
> only Son, that whoever believes in him shall not
> perish but have eternal life* (JOHN 3:16).

That statement is a familiar formula to us all—something like "two plus two equals four" or "H_2O is water."

But think about the emotions of it:

God so loved the world . . .

> *I was the one [He says] who taught Israel to
> walk . . . I drew them to me with affection and
> love. I picked them up and held them to my
> cheek . . .*
>
> > *How can I give you up, Israel? . . . My love for you
> > is too strong* (HOSEA 11:3,4,8 TEV).

" . . . *that he gave his one and only Son*," in whom He delighted (MATTHEW 12:18). We cannot imagine His unspeak-
able grief at the cross—deeper far than David's grief over his
Absalom:

> *O my son . . . my son, my son Absalom! If only I
> had died instead of you—O Absalom, my son,
> my son!* (2 SAMUEL 18:33).

Why did He do it?

> *. . . that whoever believes in him . . .*

Believe, our friend! Take Him seriously! We're not quoting these words as an invitation to salvation, but as an urging to sanctification. Open your heart. Accept to yourself this amazing, self-sacrificing, yearning, intense, eternal, God-sized love that God has for you!

> *. . . shall not perish but have eternal life—"*

in unbroken, unthreatened, pure, restful, loving, happy fellowship with Him. Starting now.

The more you study and understand the gospel of God, the more you'll begin to understand how much He really loves you.

You have eternal life at all "because of his great love for you" (EPHESIANS 2:4).

You are personally led from day to day because of His unfailing love (EXODUS 15:13).

Whether you're aware of it or not, His love surrounds you (PSALM 32:10) and supports you (PSALM 94:18).

In fact, the earth is filled with his love (PSALM 119:64): air, water, material beauty, comfort—every supply for your well-being. He loves you.

Said William James, "To some, religion exists [only] as a dull habit."[1] These people have no idea what a Christian in Western Australia meant when she recently wrote us, "When I was driving yesterday, I had tears running down my face, and I just kept saying aloud, 'You love me! You love me!' "

"Behold, what manner of love the Father hath bestowed upon us" (1 JOHN 3:1 KJV). Behold it, look at it, study it, think about it. When you do, you'll see greater wealth than the Queen of Sheba saw, who exclaimed, "I did not believe . . . until I came and saw with my own eyes" (1 KINGS 10:7).

Yesterday afternoon the two of us, writing this portion of the book together in London, took a break and wandered into St. Paul's Cathedral. (On this spot Christians have been worshiping weekly since A.D. 604!) We were barely inside the door to look up, beneath us, and around us at such breathtaking beauty in detail, proportion, and size when we were confronted by a brass plaque. It urged us to look beyond the magnificence of the cathedral to the magnificence of God. And it ended with these tender words: "As His majesty is, so is His mercy."

Yes! He is awesome, but He is so approachable.

Yes! He is Almighty God, but He is so intimately near.

He loves you.

As you read this book—

> *May the Lord direct your hearts into the love of God* (2 THESSALONIANS 3:5 KJV).

Then you'll come. You will draw close to this One who loves you so totally.

And you will stay there, *abiding in his love* (JOHN 15:9),

> *Cherishing His presence,*
> *Praising Him in His presence,*
> *Cleansed from sin in His presence,*
> *Bearing your troubles in His presence,*
> *Laughing and exulting in His presence,*
> *Feeling secure in His presence,*
> *Being without fear in His presence,*
> *Living your life, from moment to moment,*
> > *In His presence.*

3

The Capacity of God

When *God loves you—not anybody else but Almighty God—He loves you with the capacity of God.* He loves you to the utmost (JOHN 13:1).

God knew that for you and Him to be best friends in sweetest communion with each other, you needed to be cleansed of all your sins—all. "What fellowship can light have with darkness?" (2 CORINTHIANS 6:14).

So the blockbuster truth of history is that—

> *If we walk in the light, as he is in the light, we have fellowship with one another [that is, he with us and we with him], and the blood of Jesus, his Son, purifies us from all sin* (1 JOHN 1:7).

From *all* sin. God has already made you perfectly clean, perfectly acceptable, for fellowship with Him.

Seventeenth-century John Owen explains the original Hebrew meaning of ZEPHANIAH 3:17, "He will quiet you with his love":

> Literally, the Hebrew is, "He shall be silent because of his love." To rest with contentment is

expressed by being silent, that is, without grumbling and complaining. Because God's love is so full, so perfect and so absolute, it will not allow him to complain of anything in those He loves. So He is silent."[1]

When God the Father looks at you, because of the sacrifice of His Son, Jesus Christ, He just can't think of one bad thing about you. He has no complaints at all!

The same will be true of God's people Israel in their day of restoration:

> *"In those days, at that time,"*
> *declares the Lord,*
> *"search will be made for Israel's guilt,*
> *but there will be none,*
> *and for the sins of Judah,*
> *but none will be found"* (JEREMIAH 50:20).

HEBREWS 10:15–18 says the same thing about us, and that He is not ashamed of us (HEBREWS 2:11).

When God forgives you—not anybody else but Almighty God—He forgives you with the capacity of God.

But more. It isn't enough to just negatively have your sins erased; you need God's divine righteousness to be given you as your very own. And because He loves you so much, He gives it to you happily and freely. You are—

> Dressed in His righteousness alone,
> Faultless to stand before the throne![2]

Believer, you have been given Christ's own life of perfect righteousness (ROMANS 4:5). That's why God so delights in you, and why He loves to have you in His presence. He has created you for fellowship with Himself—

For your joy and for His.

For your satisfaction and for His.

For your fulfillment and for His! He calls you His "fullness" (EPHESIANS 1:23).

And He confides that glory has come to Him *through you* (JOHN 17:10). Imagine!

His love—for both you and Him to experience—is a love of rest, contentment, and delight. The Lord "rejoices in his works" (PSALM 104:31)—including you.

> He and I, in peace and glory,
>   One great comfort share:
> Mine, to be forever with Him,
>   His, that I am there![3]

In our hearts we all say, "But, but, but—!" We're painfully aware of our daily sins. As our book *Disciplines of the Heart* says, we are "both weak and wicked."[4] Even our finest deeds—what we think of as our best acts of righteousness— when measured by God's goodness are, says ISAIAH 64:6, "filthy rags." And the meaning of "filthy rags" in the original Hebrew is used feminine sanitary pads—not only loathsome but the very proof of our nonproductivity, our sterility, our emptiness.

*I know that nothing good lives in me, that is, in my
sinful nature* (ROMANS 7:18).

But God's great love for us didn't plan that our earthly
lives would just be some kind of Twilight Zone, full of ignorance, stumblings, and barrenness.

*When God saves you—not anybody else but Almighty
God—He saves you with the capacity of God.*

Old Testament priests had to offer sacrifices "day after
day . . . for the [day-after-day] sins of the people."

*But [Christ] sacrificed for [our] sins once for all when
he offered himself* (HEBREWS 7:27).

"Once for all"! He covered all the daily stuff, too. Salvation
through Christ is total, and it is God's ultimate gift of love.

May [His] unfailing love be [your] comfort (PSALM
119:76).

We have to stop and exclaim, "Is God wonderful, or
what!"

Yes, He provided for your eternal justification. But He
also provided for your moment-by-moment sanctification.
Your Father is continually cleansing you.

He saved you from your past sins "through the wash-
ing of rebirth;" but then He also saves you from your present sins through "renewal by the Holy Spirit, whom he
pours out on [you] generously" (TITUS 3:5,6).

> Oh, love of God—how rich and pure,
> How measureless and strong![5]

He who knows you best loves you most.

And His purpose is more than just to bring His sons to glory; He wants to bring *glory to His sons.*

He has more in mind than just to get you to heaven; He wants to get *heaven to you.*

He wants you to live in His joyous presence not only later, but now.

So He has provided that right now you can "approach God with freedom and confidence" (EPHESIANS 3:12). Vote against your pangs of guilt, your uneasy feelings of unworthiness!

> *We set our hearts at rest in his presence whenever our hearts condemn us. For God is greater than our hearts* (1 JOHN 3:19,20).

Hear it loud and clear: *When God cleanses you—not anybody else but Almighty God—He cleanses you with the capacity of God.*

We continually sin, but He also continually cleanses. The process is this:

> *If we confess our sins, he is faithful and just and will forgive us our sins and purify us from all unrighteousness* (1 JOHN 1:9).

We're too blind and ignorant to know all the ways we sin before our all-pure God. But when we confess the little

we know, He purifies us from *all* unrighteousness—
everything else as well!

Don't torture yourself over the difference between how
God sees you and how you see yourself. Hebrews 10:14
shows how God's love for you blends the two together in
His onflowing purposes:

> By one sacrifice he has made perfect forever
> those who are *being made holy* [day by day].

And so—

> *May God himself, the God of peace, sanctify you*
> *through and through. May your whole spirit, soul and*
> *body be preserved blameless* (1 THESSALONIANS 5:23).

When God superintends your life from here to eternity—
not anybody else but Almighty God—He superintends it with the
capacity of God. In your "now" as well as in your future, God
has not only made you accepted in His presence, He has
made you thrillingly acceptable.

> Come into His presence singing "Alleluia"
> [Praise the Lord]!

4

The Way to His Presence

Wrote Frank Laubach in his diary on January 20, 1930:

> Two years ago a profound dissatisfaction [with myself] led me to begin trying to line up my actions with the will of God about every fifteen minutes or every half hour. Other people to whom I confessed this intention said it was impossible. I judge from what I have heard that few people are really trying even that . . .[1]

In a way, who blames them? In our natural state as human beings it's silly to talk about trying to come into the presence of God. It would be like some garden worm aspiring to try out as an astronaut.

But let us give you a more reasonable illustration.

There are many places in London where we foreigners, or even Brits who are commoners, aren't allowed. Daily, especially in Westminster, we pass large, ornate gates, often gold-gilt, with brilliantly uniformed Royal Guard in front of them, standing immaculate, stony-faced, intimidating. With the rest of the common blokes we can mill around outside gawking, but we can't go in.

How much more so the Holy of Holies, where Almighty God resides!

Picture the Old Testament tabernacle, and later the temple. These were earthly copies of God's permanent dwelling place in heaven (HEBREWS 8:5; 9:24), so we'd better pay attention.

Any ordinary person was allowed up to the entrance of the outer court (LEVITICUS 1:3), but no farther—like us tourists in London.

Then the lower-echelon priests, donned in gorgeous robes of blue, purple, and scarlet, worked in the outer court and within the Holy Place, which was the front two-thirds of the tabernacle or temple (EXODUS 39:1)—like the spit-and-polish Royal Guard.

But then—

> *Behind the second curtain was a room called the Most Holy Place, which had the golden altar of incense and the gold-covered ark of the covenant. . . . Above the ark were the cherubim of the Glory. [The Glory was the actual Presence of God] . . .*
>
> *The priests entered regularly into the outer room [the Holy Place] to carry on their ministry. But only the high priest entered the inner room [the Holy of Holies], and that only once a*

> *year, and never without blood, which he offered*
> *for himself and for the sins [of] the people*
> (HEBREWS 9:3–7).

Even the consecrated priests in all their beautiful robes were never allowed to put a toe inside the silent, gorgeous, remote Place of the Presence.

No! Never!

Much less the common people.

So what makes us today think we can chatter so freely about living in the presence of God? Only—only—because of the Lord Jesus Christ. He is the final and perfect High Priest, who offered Himself to be the final and perfect sacrifice, and who entered God's presence not with the blood of animals but with His very own.

His own blood!

> *Who is this coming* [asks Isaiah] . . . *his garments*
> *stained with crimson?*
> *Who is this, robed in splendor, striding forward in*
> *the greatness of his strength?* (ISAIAH 63:1).

Jesus answers:

> *It is I, speaking in righteousness,*
> *mighty to save.*

And Isaiah asks:

> *Why are your garments red, like those of one*
> *treading the winepress?* (verse 2).

Jesus answers by describing His cross, His means of reconciling us to God and making us qualify at last to enter God's presence:

> *I have trodden the winepress alone . . .*
> *I have stained all my clothing . . .*
> *I looked, but there was no one to help,*
> *I was appalled that no one gave support,*
> *So my own arm worked salvation for me*
> (verses 3–5).

Jesus' cross is your proof of qualification. It's your personal pass! If you have accepted His love and humbly received His offer of forgiveness for all your sins, then you're invited—
> encouraged—
> > urged—
> > > *commanded* to draw near to God.

> *We have confidence to enter the Most Holy Place by the blood of Jesus, by a new and living way* (HEBREWS 10:19).

What is that new and living way, that path? "You have made known to me the path of life," sang David in PSALM 16:11. "I am the way," says Jesus in JOHN 14:6. The blood of Jesus is the secret—the path of life, the way into His presence. Then:

> *Let us draw near to God with a sincere heart in full assurance of faith* (HEBREWS 10:22).

> *Do not throw away your confidence; it will be richly rewarded* (HEBREWS 10:35).

Come!

> *Draw near to God and He will draw near to you* (JAMES 4:8 NKJV). *Come!*

5

An Explanation

Why have the two of us put so much doctrine in the first part of this book—a book about practicing the presence of God? Because doctrine must come before application.

We never saw this until recently. We were in the car listening to an old taped sermon of Dr. Martin Lloyd-Jones, preacher in London of the last generation. Dr. Lloyd-Jones said that application must flow out of doctrinal truth, that it must never stand by itself.

The thought hit us like a ton of bricks. Our current Christian generation is obsessed with application—meeting "felt needs": how to have a good marriage, how to improve your self image, how to raise kids. . . .

It dawned on us that application which doesn't flow out of doctrine is like a cut flower: it's without continuing nourishment; it's dying. "Recovery" how-to's, "success" how-to's—most are rootless, so they could be taught by Buddhists, Hindus, anybody. Application by itself isn't Christianity, and when a generation grows up which knows only application, the next generation will have lost Christianity altogether. We're living in dangerous days!

We two have been thinking a lot about this. Our generation is desperate for preachers and teachers who will get back to the great truths of the gospel: justification by faith, sanctification, imputed righteousness, prophecy, heaven and hell. The truths that occupy great space in God's Word should occupy great space in our concerns, and they are those which establish, strengthen, settle us.

The book of Romans has 11 chapters of doctrine followed by five of application. Ephesians first has three chapters of doctrine, then three of how-to's. Philippians has two and two; Colossians has two and two.

Please hear us carefully! "Practicing God's presence," unless it flows out of the nourishing, deep-rooted truths of our Christian faith, becomes purely experiential, shallow, and eventually silly.

What you believe about God—your theology—is what shapes and defines the real you. More than what how-to seminars teach you (although they can be helpful), how you behave in marriage, raise children, and generally function as a person *will flow out of your knowledge of God and your life with Him.*

Our friend Roy Castle was one of England's great and much-loved comedian-actor-entertainers. Then cancer struck him down. He died a few months ago.

When you can't do shows anymore, when you can't accept television dates, when you can't travel and make people laugh, when you can't function in any of the old familiar patterns—what then?

Roy's dear believing wife Fiona was at his bedside at the end, when he was lying motionless in a coma. But suddenly he raised himself in bed and said in a firm, victorious voice, "I believe in Jesus Christ!" Roy's final statement about himself was his Christian faith. All the clothing of his life had been piece by piece stripped away, and the real Roy Castle was left exposed.

Friend, one day soon you will answer before God as to how you grew in two ways: in grace (in His atmosphere, His aroma, His personality) and in the knowledge of Him (2 PETER 3:18).

Remember: Every day, every hour, you're writing your own autobiography.

6

An Application

Sometimes the two of us get out of gas; so do you. Two days ago, here in California, we put in an 18-hour day that included driving 60 miles through heavy traffic, broadcasting several radio programs, and participating in many intense meetings. But when we fell exhausted into a strange bed that night we were still blessedly "in Christ."

Last night we went to an early movie—a rare, harmless, deliciously romantic movie, while we hugged and had popcorn and diet Cokes—and followed it with a light supper in a charming place. Last night, too, we were wonderfully "in Christ."

In recent weeks we've had some battles with sleeplessness, taking off weight, and shingles! But whether our eyes ache or our tummies growl or we itch, our position "in Christ" never, never changes.

Being in Christ is doctrinal truth, and there's nothing more sustaining and steadying than doctrinal truth. For instance, JOHN 14 gives you doctrinal truth, and then JOHN 15 gives you the application which flows out of that doctrine.

In JOHN 14:20 Jesus tells you, "You are in me, and I am in you." (And He is describing your relationship with Him in exactly the same way He has earlier described in verses 10 and 11 His own awesome relationship within the divine Trinity!)

That is doctrinal truth—unchangeable, no matter how you feel or what your circumstances.

Then chapter 15 shifts to application: "Now that you know as a settled fact that you are in Christ, make it your experience to consciously settle down in Him. Make yourself at home in Him. *Abide in Christ.* By your own deliberate choice, by an act of your will, develop the holy habit of being consciously aware of Him and drawing on Him, from moment to moment."

Verses 4 and 5 say abide in Him; verses 9 and 10 say abide in His love. Those two are synonymous, don't you think?

Abiding in Christ isn't automatic behavior for every Christian, or Jesus wouldn't command it. No, we all realize what it's like to know *theoretically* that we're God's children but then live all day long like orphans—fussing, worrying, struggling in our own strength.

A few years ago we two were in the financial crunch of our life. All our savings were stripped away, and we were in danger of losing our last material holding, our home. Many times in the past we might have fussed—but *God was near.*

We talked about it together: "We have the Lord; we have each other; we have our family and friends, all so precious; we have our ministry. What if we live the rest of our lives in a rented apartment? We'll still be so rich!"

We actually never lost our home—but think about it:

Where is Christ? He's in you.

Where are you? You're in Him.

Then how should you live? Resting in Him, loving Him, happy in Him, abiding in Him, drawing life and strength continually from Him as a branch draws life and strength from the vine.

Just constantly, consciously, *staying there*. And enjoying to the full where you are.

Obstacles to His Presence

Why, O Lord, do you stand afar off?
Why do you hide yourself in times
of trouble?

—Psalm 10:1

7

Our Perception of God's Unreality

You may be saying, "I can't draw near to someone I can't see! God isn't visible!" It's like the story of the little girl sobbing during a thunderstorm at night, "But I want somebody with skin on!"

It's true that God is invisible, but *so is the immortal part of you.* You know very well that the real "you" isn't just your body. Your body is purely temporary, and soon it's going to fade off the scene altogether.

The two of us were talking about this yesterday. "Certainly after living together all these years and seeing our bodies change," we said, "we don't think of 'Ray' or 'Anne' in terms of what we're looking at. We have to add, we're crazy about our bodies, too! But—no doubt about it—it's the real person inside that we've loved for so long."

The real you is the part of you that thinks, loves, gets irritated, hopes, desires, rejoices, mourns, wills, cares—and that's true also with God.

Frederick Lawrence Knowles said it in old-fashioned English:

This body is my house—it isn't I;
Herein I sojourn till in that far sky
I lease a dwelling place that's built to last
When all the carpentry of time is past.[1]

When you trade your physical body for your resurrection body, the essential you will still be you; and it is this conscious, invisible you which has full capacity right now to interact with a conscious, invisible God.

Speak to Him, thou, for He heareth, and
        Spirit with spirit can meet;
Closer is He than breathing, and
        Nearer than hands and feet.[2]

He is always here, and He is always simultaneously elsewhere!

"Am I only a God nearby," declares the Lord,
    "and not a God far away?
Can anyone hide in secret places
    so that I cannot see him?" declares the Lord.
"Do I not fill heaven and earth?" (JEREMIAH 23:23,24).

Writes Skevington Wood:

We can never talk about God behind His back. We cannot speak of God in His absence . . . The God who is being discussed is also there. The attitude people take to Him can never be merely theoretical. To deny Him is to spite Him to His face.[3]

We can remember times when we tried to get a spoonful of food into one of our babies' mouths—food that was nourishing and vitamin-packed, definitely good for our kid. *We* knew that, but *she* didn't know that; she only thought she might not like it. So there we sat, at an impasse. The spoonful was right at her mouth, but the mouth was a hard, tight line, impossible to penetrate. The food was right there, but she wasn't receiving it, so it wasn't doing her any good.

So God is with the Christian. He promised He would be; He is good to His word; He is not going away. But if His presence isn't received it won't do the Christian any good; he'll go on fretting and struggling and being fearful and trying to do things his own.

"Here I am!" Christ says in Revelation 3:20. And at this very moment as you sit reading, He says to you, "Where you are, here I am, too."

> Here I am! I stand at the door [of your conscious acceptance of my presence] and knock. If [you] hear my voice and open the door, I will come in and eat with [you] and [you] with me—

An act of friendship and fellowship.

8

Our Pressures and Pace

The fast actions of most Christians blur their images so we can't see them very well. And neither can they see us, or see God.

When you're driving down a superhighway at 65 miles an hour you don't see much of what's happening around you. And even if your best friend is at your side you can't have deep conversations; you have to stay alert to the road.

Modern life is like that. It's terribly fast-paced, complex, pressured, and pressurizing. So we Christians are usually strained, burdened, breathless Mad Hatters, living our duty-driven lives while furtively glancing at our watches to keep up.

Writes Thomas Kelly:

> The times for the deeps of the silences of the heart seem so few. And in guilty regret we must postpone till next week that deeper life of unshaken composure in the Holy Presence, where we sincerely know our true home is, for *this* week is much too full.[1]

" You have made KNOWN
TO Me the path of Life;
You will Fill Me
with Joy IN your
PRESENCE, With
eTERNAL pleASUReS
AT your Right HAnd
PSALm 16:11

The ONe Who FeAns IS

NoT Made penfect in Love
    1 John 4:18

If this is how you feel, don't immediately change any-thing outward. Don't blame your panic on how the world is. Or don't give false explanations that you're put upon, that it's not your fault, that there are simply many needs that have to be met. The answer doesn't lie in wishing you could retreat to the horse-and-buggy days, or dreaming of a move to the country, or framing a speech in your mind to ask for more time off, or taking a pill. The need isn't physical escape.

Think, Christian, *who is with you.* Right here. Right now. Inside, underneath, overshadowing, *with.* Think how much He loves you, how concerned He is. Think of His cleansing forgiveness. Think of His tender care. Think of His plans for your future.

Stop right now and say, "God loves me."
Emphasize the first word: *"God* loves me."
Emphasize the middle one: "God *loves* me!" Think about it.
Emphasize the last one: "God loves *me!"*

Life is always revolutionized from within. Winning the lottery doesn't do it; *living is between your ears.*

Think about God. Think about His pace. (One reli-gious philosopher has decided that God moves at about three miles an hour!)

But don't think most about His pace; think most about His *grace.* The two of us are learning a little more about His moment-by-moment fellowship; we want to know it better. And we're discovering that it's not *work* which debilitates, it's only a wrong attitude toward work. In fact, it's not *living* which debilitates, but only a wrong attitude toward living.

> *There remains, then, a Sabbath-rest for the people of God; for anyone who enters God's rest also rests from his own work, just as God did from his. Let us, therefore, make every effort to enter that rest* (HEBREWS 4:9–11).

"Make every effort to . . . rest." We activists don't naturally rest. We live in the presence not of God but of our problems and our situations; so we tense up and we press too hard.

> *Find rest, O my soul, in God alone* (PSALM 62:5).

> *We set our hearts at rest in his presence* (1 JOHN 3:19).

> *He who dwells in the shelter of the Most High will rest in the shadow of the Almighty* (PSALM 91:1).

Practicing the presence of God isn't something to add to your already busy schedule. It doesn't take *more* of your time, it takes *all* of your time. It's what you do while you do whatever you're doing.

But as you dwell in the presence of God, your life will gradually rearrange itself. You'll find that some activities don't seem appropriate anymore, or have simply gotten boring, and that without much effort they'll drop away. Other

activities will take over; they will become your longing and
your delight.

Jacob was engrossed in traveling, engrossed in the pain
and worry of bad relationships—engrossed in *living*, and all
of it at a pell-mell pace.

Then he had a dream. When he woke up he exclaimed, "Surely the Lord is in this place, and I was not
aware of it!" (GENESIS 28:16).

When Jacob accepted into his life an awareness of the
immediacy of God, he was revolutionized. And his life
began to move *up*—slowly at times, and with regressions—
but humbly and surely *up* as he lived with God.

Still, how could he ever have guessed the status, the
privileges, by the end? (We all have to read our lives like
Hebrew: backward.) By age 130 Jacob was walking, limp-
ing, with his face toward the sunset and toward the glory.

And his name had become Israel.

9

Our Pride

If you desire a happy, loving, well-synchronized relation-ship with God, there are six facts you need to acknowledge and absorb. They will help you understand who He is and who you are; it's important not to get the two confused!

1. **All power is of God.**

> *Power and might are in your hand, and no one can withstand you"* (2 Chronicles 20:6).

There is no worthy power, no ability, apart from God; and any power, any ability, you have is simply what He chooses to give you. Say yes to that right now!

2. **All money and possessions are of God**.

> *Every animal in the forest is mine [says God], and the cattle on a thousand hills . . . If I were hungry I would not tell you, for the world is mine and all that is in it* (Psalm 50: 10,12).
>
> *All things were created by him and for him* (Colossians 1:16).

No one owns anything apart from God. Any material thing you may have—salary, savings, inheritances, gifts—anything you may temporarily possess is what God chooses, temporarily, to lend you. Say yes to that right now.

3. All wisdom is of God.

> *Oh, the depth of the riches of the wisdom and*
> *knowledge of God!*
> *How unsearchable his judgments,*
> *and his paths beyond tracing out!*
> *Who has known the mind of the Lord?*
> *Or who has been his counselor? . . .*
> *For from him and through him and to him are*
> *all things.*
> *To him be the glory forever! Amen* (ROMANS 11:33–36).

There is no wisdom apart from God. Any wisdom you ever have is simply the wisdom He chooses to give to you. Say yes to that right now.

> *The Lord gives wisdom* (PROVERBS 2:6).

> *If any of you lacks wisdom, he should ask God* (JAMES 1:5).

4. All energy is of God.

> *[He sustains] all things by his powerful word* (HEBREWS 1:3).

> *If . . . he withdrew his spirit and breath, all mankind*
> *would perish together* (JOB 34:14,15).

There is no energy (no *dunamis*, in the Greek, from which
we get our word "dynamite") apart from God. Any energy
you have is simply what He chooses to let you temporarily
possess. Say yes to that right now.

> *The Lord is the everlasting God . . .*
> *He will not grow tired or weary* (ISAIAH 40:28).

And Ultimate Energy can at any time choose to impart energy to His people:

> *He gives strength to the weary*
>   *and increases the power of the weak.*
> *Even youths grow tired and weary,*
>   *and young men stumble and fall;*
> *but those who hope in the Lord*
>   *will . . . run and not grow weary,*
>   *they will walk and not be faint* (ISAIAH 40:29–31).

5. All life, all health, is of God.

> *In him [is] life* (JOHN 1:4).

> *As the Father has life in himself, so he has granted the*
> *Son to have life in himself* (JOHN 5:26).

There is no life, no health, apart from God. Your physical
life and health are gifts from Him, and if you have spiritual

life and health, they too are His gifts. Say yes to that right now.

> *Listen closely to my words . . .*
> *Keep them within your heart;*
> *for they are life to those who find them*
> *and health to a man's whole body* (PROVERBS 4:20–22).

6. All forgiveness is of God.

Who can forgive sins but God alone? (MARK 2:7).

With you there is forgiveness (PSALM 130:4).

There is no forgiveness apart from God. If we try to "forgive ourselves" we're still guilty, because we have no authority to forgive sins. Only the sinless One, only the pure Judge of all, qualifies to forgive.

If you're forgiven it's because you have accepted forgiveness on His terms—through the death and resurrection of His Son Jesus for your sins, and because God has chosen to forgive you. Say yes to that right now.

The simple conclusion to these six simple facts is this: *Pride cannot coexist with God.* In ISAIAH 42:8 He thunders:

> *I am the Lord; that is my name!*
> *I will not give my glory to another.*

A clandestine spirit of rivalry with God—love for self, self-awareness, self-glorification—is enmity-to-the-death against love for God, God-awareness, God-glorification.

Beware of spiritual strutting! Beware of seeking publicity as one who lives in God's presence. Don't parade it; don't force it on others; don't even talk about it—"just do it."

Bonhoeffer speaks of "the proper hiddenness of Christian behavior." Practicing His presence is a humble, modest thing; it can't be measured or displayed. That means there's no competing for first place, no embarrassment over coming in last. We're simply abiding in the love of God, which takes no credit to ourselves.

And we do this only by the gracious work of the Holy Spirit. He Himself must continually tutor us, discipline us, simplify us, give us discomfort when we offend Him, gently lead us along the way.

> *Ray*: I remember as a young sailor in the U.S. Navy, walking alone on the streets of New York City. And I remember feeling absolutely assaulted by temptation. It seemed as if there was a battle in the air directly over my head, and the devil was determined to get me and cut me down.
>
> And I can remember as if it were yesterday how the presence of the Lord was so real and so precious, He seemed just to lift me right up and out of the oppression! I was still a young sailor walking alone on the city streets, but I had a strong sense of being wonderfully rescued.

Living close to God is His work alone. In fact, the closer we draw to all His riches, the more we'll be aware of our own poverty—but it won't matter. We plunge into God, swallowed up by Him, happy in His love, His tenderness, His kindness, His goodness, and we are "lost in wonder, love, and praise."[1] The awesomeness of the Lord God will press in upon us, unfiltered and powerful, and we will have no choice but to follow Him and enjoy Him.

We won't be applauded for this, and we won't applaud ourselves. But we will learn more and more the amazing truth that—

> *We, who with unveiled faces all reflect the Lord's glory, are being transformed into his likeness with ever-increasing glory, which comes from the Lord, who is the Spirit* (2 CORINTHIANS 3:18).

Will this process in you take time? Probably. The rate of growth is up to God. Impatience and pushiness, even in spiritual things, is the fruit of pride. (Brother Lawrence spoke of not trying to advance faster than grace!) "It is God who works in you to will and to act according to his good purpose" (PHILIPPIANS 2:13).

Think about how God grows His roses and His redwood trees. Note at what pace He is bringing about His new heavens and new earth! Thomas Kelly speaks of "the Cosmic patience of God."

Let's happily humble ourselves and get in step with Him.

The Scriptures call it "waiting on the Lord" and "hoping in God."

10

Our Unyielding Wills

How much precious time and energy is wasted because our wills insist on our going our own ways in our own powers! It's like rowing upstream, stubbornly resisting the fact that there is a motor in the rear of the boat.

Have you taken seriously God's flat statement in 2 PETER 1:3?

> *His divine power has given us everything we need for life and godliness.*

"I am with you," He assures you over and over "—with you always for all your requirements." Believe it!

The Gospel of Matthew begins with the announcement of His name: "Immanuel—which means 'God with us' " (1:23). It ends with the announcement of His mode of operating: "I am with you always, to the very end of the age" (28:20).

Then what is the real blockage? It's our wills.

You can know the truth, discuss it, study it, praise it—but now let it touch you deeply enough to surrender to it and live it.

Educators say that true education hasn't taken place until there is changed behavior. You won't know the presence of God unless you yield and accept it as the Fact of your life.

He is already with you. Lay down your defenses, then, and acknowledge His reality, confess your sins, submit to Him, receive Him anew.

Then—get ready for a surprise—do you know how He'll respond? He will party with you! That's His style.

> *He calls his friends and neighbors together and*
> *says, "Rejoice with me; I have found my lost sheep"*
> (LUKE 15:5,6).

Are you shocked? Do you think of God as always somber and austere? God is gregarious, and when the sins that separate us from Him have been dealt with, He says it's time to celebrate!

In the Scriptures, when God-fearing people come humbly and thankfully into His presence, what happens?

> *Moses and Aaron, Nadab and Abihu, and the*
> *seventy elders of Israel went up [the mountain]*
> *and saw the God of Israel. Under his feet*
> *was something like a pavement made of sap-*
> *phire, clear as the sky itself. But God did not*
> *raise his hand against these leaders of the*
> *Israelites; they saw God, and they ate and*
> drank (EXODUS 24:9–11).

Or this time:

> Then [King] David said to the whole assembly,
> "Praise the Lord your God.' " So they all praised
> the Lord . . . They made sacrifices . . . They ate
> and drank with great joy in the presence of the
> Lord that day (1 CHRONICLES 29:20–22).

When the prodigal son humbled himself and came back repentant into the presence of his father, what does Jesus say happened? The father gave him new clothes and jewelry and threw a party with music and dancing (LUKE 15:17–25).

How did Christ celebrate His postresurrection reunion with His disciples? With a seaside breakfast of broiled fish (JOHN 21:1–12). Delicious and fun!

And what does He want to do with you personally when you open wide your heart to Him? Says Revelation 3:20, He wants the two of you to sit down and have a meal together.

But now, here's a warning. *Don't mistake your open access to Him as "easy believism."*

Jesus told a parable of a king throwing a wonderful banquet for honored guests—

> But they paid no attention and went off—one to his
> field, another to his business (MATTHEW 22:5).

And so, with his heart full of lovingkindness, the king threw open his palace doors and invited in the riffraff from the streets (you and us) to enjoy his beautiful party. So far we have a lovely picture of God's grace.

But one smart aleck who came to the dinner defied the dress code. Then what happened to the host's happy party mood?

> *[He] told the attendants, "Tie him hand and foot, and throw him outside into the darkness, where there will be weeping and gnashing of teeth"* (verse 13).

The God with whom we have to do is infinitely kind, but He will not flatter. He is still God, and we must come to Him on His terms. We must humbly accept the new clothing of His righteousness and His way of living. We understand the danger of any alternative.

Practicing the presence of God isn't just showing up at a dinner party with an unyielded will to get in on the fun. God is holy. He demands repentance, which is a total change of direction. We cannot enter as our unchanged selves. There are no gate crashers.

The prodigal son tending pigs didn't try to improve his conditions; he made a wrenching break with his own rebellion and went back to his father.

Jonah, too, tried to flee from the presence of the Lord (JONAH 1:3 NKJV) and ended up in the belly of a great fish. Jonah, too, was in the wrong place, and he too made a 180-degree change of direction back to his God.

Understand who it is with whom you're dealing! If you are Almighty God's—if you belong to Him through the great price of the cross of Christ—then for that reason alone He will never tie you hand and foot and toss you out.

But a great salvation demands a great response. You are God's, and He loves you too much to let you get by with boredom, staleness, carnality, distance. He will put you in a pigpen or a fish! Only a careless God would let you continue unrebuked.

Self-will doesn't give up easily; your ego may give you a real battle. Surrender and come with tears, if tears are what it takes—

But surrender and come.

It is only as you stand inside the door of the great feast—humbled, grateful, obedient—that you will know for yourself that "at his right hand there are pleasures forevermore" (Psalm 16:11 kjv).

At the culmination of history there will be the wedding supper of the Lamb (Revelation 19:9). Expect it to be a fabulous event! But the heart-melting surprise of the whole affair may be this:

> . . .*When he comes, I tell you the truth, he will dress himself to serve, will have them recline at the table, and will come and wait on them* (Luke 12:37)!

Hold this to your heart; it is a mystery of the universe: God's greatest gift to His beloved people has always been, is now, and will always be, *Himself.*

11

✦▬▬✦▬✦▬▬✦

Our Distractions

Did you ever try to write a book? Probably your biggest challenge wasn't to think what you wanted to say, or gather and organize your material—it was just to sit down and do it. There were a thousand distractions! For us, too.

Getting to anything worthwhile means getting past the obstacles. We see four obvious distractions from practicing the presence of God.

First distraction: our own sins. Satan, "the accuser of our brothers" who accuses us "day and night" (REVELATION 12:10), would love to discourage and defeat you. Resist him with the Word of God, as Jesus did in Luke 4, and he will flee from you (JAMES 4:7).

What word will overcome him? Try the powerful weapon of Romans chapter 6. Study it, revel in it! It says, "sin shall not be your master" (verse 14). In His presence our enemy stumbles and falls (PSALM 27:2; JOHN 18:6), and our sins have lost their sting (1 CORINTHIANS 15:56,57).

Wrote Brother Lawrence in his diary:

> When I fail in my duty I simply admit my faults, saying to God, "I shall never do otherwise if You leave

me to myself. It is You who must stop my falling. . . ."
After such praying I allow myself no further uneasi-
ness about my faults.

In all things we should act toward God with the
greatest simplicity, speaking to Him frankly and
plainly and imploring His assistance. . . .[1]

I am keenly aware of my faults, but I am not dis-
couraged by them. When I have confessed my faults
to the Lord, I peacefully resume my usual practice of
love and adoration to Him. . . .

We ought, without any anxiety, to expect the par-
don of our sins from the blood of the Lord Jesus
Christ; our only endeavor should be to love him with
all our hearts.[2]

Here is authentic Christian theology. This isn't the attitude of an orphaned waif, cringing at the door of the castle
not knowing whether he is welcome or not. This is the
mindset of the son of the king, who is aware that he is often
disobedient but who nevertheless expects to be pardoned.
In fact, his father's very graciousness makes the son hate to
displease him! But basically he knows that he belongs, that
he is accepted, that the riches of the kingdom are his, and
that, *because of who his father is,* he lives a life of privilege and
honor.

The blessing of studying Brother Lawrence is in seeing that here was no spoiled brat, taking advantage of this
marvelous relationship; that would have been odious. No,

he just humbly and continually sought to please his Father and revel in their love for each other.

Second distraction from practicing the presence of God: bad theology. Untaught Christians think of God only as 'way up there in heaven. Meanwhile they're cleaning, shopping, paying bills, driving, at their desks—doing immediate duties and aware of immediate problems, immediate pressures, immediate fears.

God seems far away, but what seems close? Humanistic self-help programs of every kind. They're right at their elbows, promising solutions.

But, friend, *God is closer.* Believe it! "In Him we live and move and have our being" (ACTS 17:28). If you'll hear Him, Christ says:

> *Come to me, all you who are weary and burdened, and I will give you rest. . . . Learn from me* (MATTHEW 11:28,29).
>
> *Peace I leave with you; my peace I give you. I do not give to you as the world gives. Do not let your hearts be troubled and do not be afraid* (JOHN 14:27).

To believers only, says COLOSSIANS 1:27, God is willing to make known the mystery "which is Christ in you, the hope of glory." Not the hope of mere healing or help, but glory!

Horizontal solutions are always inferior. Bad theology lowers you, demeans you. It will tempt you to turn away from the castle thinking you're not good enough. Of course you're not good enough! That's why you marvel with humility and gratitude and awe that God has totally forgiven you and cleansed you and invited you to come close.

Distraction from God's presence number three: sudden bad news, sudden interruptions, a sudden calamity. The instinct for self-preservation may make you turn away to face the problem. God doesn't despise you for this. Remember:

> *As a father has compassion on his children,*
> *so the Lord has compassion on those who fear him*
> (PSALM 103:13).

When your usual style is to "fear Him," trust Him, rely on Him, He knows that very soon you'll be drawn back again. You both know that He is your "refuge and strength, an ever present help in trouble" (PSALM 46:1). In the worst of your calamities *He is there*, immediately with you.

King Nebuchadnezzar threw three believers into a fiery furnace. So when he looked in, he—

> *leaped to his feet in amazement . . . He said, "Look! I*
> *see four men walking around in the fire, unbound and*
> *unharmed, and the fourth looks like a son of the gods"*
> (DANIEL 3:24,25).

The fourth was even more: He was *the* Son of *the* God! And the psalmist David said:

Even though I walk
through the valley of the shadow of death,
I will fear no evil, for you are with me (PSALM 23:4).

Ray: We have a dear friend, Jim. Years ago Jim stumbled drunk into our church, and people were kind to him. So the next Sunday he came back sober, and when I preached he accepted the gospel, and he grew. We became friends.

Eventually our buddy Jim's smoking caught up with him, and he developed cancer of the throat. Surgery removed his voice box, and for the last several years Jim has been without sound.

But the cancer had crept down his chest, down into his sternum. Jim is dying. His 200-pound frame is now 110 pounds. Jim has never married, and his parents, brother, and sister are all gone; he lives alone, with not one close relative in this world.

We go to see him. His Bible is all marked up, and he is always ready to show a verse he's just found.

How can I repay the Lord
for all his goodness to me? [asks PSALM 116.]
I will lift up the cup of salvation
and call upon the name of the Lord.
I will fulfill my vows to the Lord
in the presence of all his people (verses 12–14).

When Jim has the strength, he takes Christian tapes and walks to the neighborhood supermarket.

He gives them away to any takers, and if they'll give him time, he writes on a pad how good Christ is and that He loves them. The neighborhood people have gotten to know Jim—Jim's kindness, Jim's exuberance—and as a result several have been saved! Voiceless Jim has taken the cup of salvation and is joyfully witnessing of God's goodness.

What is this power in Jim's life? The other day when we were in his room he wrote on his pad, "The Lord is right here with me, in this very room. I've never been so happy."

> The longer I have been a Christian [writes Dr. Sinclair Ferguson] the more I have come to see how central this simple truth is. In many ways it is the heart of the Gospel—"Immanuel, God with us!" It is also the most basic reality of the Christian's experience.[3]

Distraction from His presence number four: simply the hunch that being continually aware of His immediacy seems too intense, too exhausting. It sounds like a lot of work. A burden.

Really? A bird's wings add weight to his body, but they don't weigh him down. Just the opposite: They lift him, they make him soar. God's presence will be your support and your strength.

The two of us travel and speak at conferences almost half of each month, and in the giving of ourselves, along with jet lag, we can sometimes get pretty tired. Then we remember what our friend Kent Hughes says: that most souls are won by tired Christians; the best sermons are preached by tired pastors; the best youth camps are run by tired youth workers; the world is being evangelized by tired missionaries. Oswald Sanders writes, "The world is run by tired people"!

It's no big deal to be tired. In and through people like you, God still gets His work done with great glory—and payday comes later.

But in all your living, realize that you don't hold onto Him; He holds you, and He lifts you. His power becomes your wings.

The merest breeze will bear you up.

The heights will become your accustomed place.

Questions
About
His Presence

12

Is This Some
Out-of-Body Experience?

The two of us are such plain, simple, ordinary people that if
you're not some spiritual giant either, maybe you can learn
from us.

We've never had a single ecstatic experience. The voice
of God has never been audible to us. We know absolutely
nothing about God saying, "Ray and Anne, here's what I
want you to do . . ."

For the life of us, we can't think why this would be
necessary or how it could enhance our spiritual experience.
Now if others get chills down their backs or hear some
thrilling voice coming to them, they're in very exciting
company: Elijah (1 KINGS 19:12,13), Paul (2 CORINTHIANS
12:1–6), and John (REVELATION 1:10–17). God is God, and
He can communicate to anyone any way He wishes.

But if He came in a vision or if He spoke out loud to
the two of us or to anyone else, would He give truth other
than what He has already revealed to His total church
through His Holy Scriptures? No! Just like you, we have
the Bible:

How firm a foundation, ye saints of the Lord,
    Is laid for your faith in His excellent Word!
What more can He say than to you He hath
    said. . . .?[1]

And just like you, we have the Holy Spirit:

> *The anointing which you received from Him abides in*
> *you, and you have no need for anyone to teach you;*
> *but . . .* His anointing teaches you about all things,
> *and is true and is not a lie"* (1 JOHN 2:27 NASB).

To tell you the truth, we're glad we've had no extra-sensational experiences of God's presence; it would make readers of this book feel they'd gotten Grade B treatment if their experiences couldn't match ours! Desiring to practice the presence of God isn't waiting for something to happen which will make any of us say "wow"—something we can hardly wait to tell everybody else.

That's why it seems healthy to us to lean on the doctrine of the presence, the solid rock of truth concerning His presence and its lovely availability. And then, in whatever way the Lord commands you, feel free to strike that doctrinal rock as Moses struck the rock in EXODUS 17:6, and the water of nourishing, blessed, even thrilling experiences will flow out. But don't strike it in impatience or self-will, as Moses did in NUMBERS 20:9–11; don't demand that God meet you on your terms, according to your own idea of how it should happen.

Confidence in the rock-solid promise of His continual presence (MATTHEW 28:20) is what will strengthen and steady you in the down times when you "feel" nothing at all. Know the doctrine! You can always trust sound doctrine; you can't always trust experience.

> *Anne:* For many years I've been writing out my daily prayers. Let me read to you from April 25, 1974:
>
> > O God! Have You left us to wander on our own? . . . Where are You, Lord? How long will You wait without a breakthrough? . . . Lord, come to us!
>
> But listen to three months later, July 23, 1974. I was purring along again, aware of His presence, comfortable and happy:
>
> > Father, You comfort me. You're on schedule, Lord—moving, strong, sure. Thank You that I'm in Your plan! I want to please You! Help me to live each day wisely. Show me how to spend each precious moment of time. I love You.
>
> But the worst time in my life was yet to come. You know how sometimes college students go through a time of questioning God's existence? That never hit me until I was 50, and it lasted a whole week:
>
> > I have cried buckets this week, with the horror that atheists must feel. I have known insecurity that I've never known before. I have cried, "Where

am I? Who am I? I don't know anything anymore!"

The turning point came when Ray said, "I
don't know how to help you, my dear Anne. I feel
so helpless! But, study your Bible about it . . ."
[And doctrine rescued me!] I started in at
Genesis . . . How the promises and assurances
came flooding around me! How You comforted
me! How ready You were to meet me and reas-
sure me of Your constant, faithful tender mercies
and loving care! . . .

And it was over.

My writings like these—sometimes feeling Him near,
sometimes not—remind me of the beginning and ending of
Psalm 10. The psalmist starts out:

> *Why, O Lord, do you stand afar off?*
> *Why do you hide yourself in times of trouble?*

And he ends,

> *You hear, O Lord, the desire of the afflicted;*
> *You encourage them, and you listen to their cry.*

The two of us love this prayer of Ralph Cushman's:

> Thou knowest that sometimes the shadows are
> very deep, that sometimes the very stars go out
> and God seems so far away. In these moments

and hours of darkness remind us, dear Christ, of
the certainty of Thy presence.

> "When darkness veils His lovely face
> I rest on His unchanging grace . . .
> On Christ, the solid Rock, I stand!"

Oh, may we do this! And whatever may be
the cause of our gloom—the weariness of our
flesh, the sudden descent of sorrow, the disap-
pointment of cherished hopes—grant us in these
hours of temptation the power to go on walking
in the paths of righteousness and peace, until the
clouds break and the light comes and the glory of
the Lord shines through.[2]

13

Is the Practice of God's Presence Escapism?

Is turning your face toward God turning your back on reality? What about the sin, suffering, and death all around us?

We two read through the Bible every year, and as we thought about this question we came to ISAIAH 14. This chapter describes Satan's final demise, and the world's resultant peace and rest, as if all of it had already happened. It reminded us again of the importance of perspective.

From God's point of view the pains and struggles of sin are agonizingly real but temporary, and the victories and joys of righteousness are long-range, beginning now with every believer and stretching even into eternity.

> For a brief moment I abandoned you [says Almighty God],
>   but with deep compassion I will bring you back.
> In a surge of anger
>   I hid my face from you for a moment,
> but with everlasting kindness
>   I will have compassion on you (ISAIAH 54:7,8).

That's God's style: Among the annual feasts of Israel, mourning over sin lasted one day only (LEVITICUS 23:26–32), while the happy celebration of tabernacles lasted a week (LEVITICUS 23:33– 43).

That principle doesn't cool down hell! It doesn't mean that God's anger isn't real. Indeed, His wrath is the most terrifying of all terrors. PSALM 29 says, for instance, that the voice of God breaks cedars, shakes the desert, twists oaks, and strips forests bare; and JEREMIAH 25:30 says that when His patience finally runs out—

The Lord will roar from on high.

And in that awful "day of the Lord" He will force the rebellious to drink the cup of His wrath to its dregs, until they stagger and go mad (JEREMIAH 25:15,16).

Grace will have ceased:

I will allow no pity or mercy or compassion to keep me from destroying them (JEREMIAH 13:14).

The same God who comforts believers also predicts dreadful judgment for unbelievers.

Consider therefore the kindness and sternness of God: sternness to those who fell, but kindness to you, provided that you continue in his kindness (ROMANS 11:22).

In LUKE 19:12–27 Jesus taught by parable the difference between these two sides of God: His kindness and His sternness. He said some of the servants of a certain king invested the king's money well because they expected a reward—and they were right. They counted on his kind side, and to them he was kind.

But one servant said he looked on the king as "a hard man," and only stashed away his entrustment. To him the king said, "I will judge you by your own words," and he put him to death.

> *Is it not from the mouth of the Most High that both*
> *calamities and good things come?* (LAMENTATIONS 3:38).

No, practicing God's presence isn't escapism. Those who move in close to be taught by the Lord and live near to Him come to know that He is not some kindly old grandfather who lets his creation get away with murder because he can't confront evil. And they also know there are not two equal powers—God and the devil, one good and one bad, one responsible for sugar and spice and everything nice and the other responsible for snips and snails and puppy dogs' tails.

The Word of God is clear, and it makes clear-eyed believers. We know that there is only one sovereign God, a God who is kind and good, a God who is responsible for all things and who makes all things—good things and bad things—ultimately work together for good (ROMANS 8:28):

> *See now that I myself am He!*
> *There is no god beside me.*

I put to death and I bring to life,
I have wounded and I will heal"
(DEUTERONOMY 32:39).

I am the Lord, and there is no other.
I form light and create darkness,
I bring prosperity and create disaster (ISAIAH 45:6,7).

The Lord brings death and makes alive;
he brings down to the grave and raises up.
The Lord sends poverty and wealth;
he humbles and he exalts (1 SAMUEL 2:6,7).

Think about the prophet Jeremiah, who in a terrible day was filled with God's Spirit and lived in His presence. Jeremiah was caught in the devastating collapse of Jerusalem, the collapse of his own country of Israel, and the collapse of the only national testimony of the true God at that time. And he physically went through much of the same suffering as his wicked countrymen, even to being carried off into exile in Egypt.

And yet Jeremiah, through his tears, rested at peace in the overriding truth of the goodness and love of his God:

Yet this I call to mind,
and therefore I have hope . . .
The Lord is good to those whose hope is in him,
to the one who seeks him (LAMENTATIONS 3:21,25).

For the believer, says Eugene Peterson, "Deeper and stronger than our illness is our cure."[1]

There is a simplicity which God wants to give you, Christian, which isn't naiveté. It isn't "ignorance [which] is bliss." It isn't the simplicity of a child who doesn't know enough to be burdened with life's problems, or the simplicity of the mentally retarded.

It is the simplicity of maturity in God. Get through the adolescence of worry, fretting, over-busyness, over-self-consciousness. Don't spend your life as one more case of arrested development.

Maturity is getting beyond all that to the long-range view: It is the simplicity of letting God be God.

Said our son Ray Jr. recently, when we were listening to him preach:

> A strong theology of a strong God is the only theology worthy of Him, and the only realistic theology. . . .
> Human opposition counts for nothing. God has already factored it into His glory. He will ultimately use it to make His glory more fully visible and more admired than ever.

To seek to police the world's rebellions until they leave us angry, frustrated, and pessimistic is pure pride, assuming a role which only God can handle. Or to bear the world's sufferings until they crush us—that, too, is assuming a role which belongs only to God. Yes, we weep with those who weep, we give to those in need, and we do all He asks of us to lift and to help; Jesus commended the Good Samaritan (LUKE 10).

But mostly, in childlike faith we look to Jesus. We understand that spiritual warfare was initiated in the heavenlies and that ultimately it is in that arena where God Himself will triumph. We wait for Him. We hope in Him. We trust Him.

And in the meantime, amazingly—

> *[He] prepares a table before [us]*
> *In the presence of [our] enemies* (PSALM 23:5).

Food and drink, fellowship and rest, right in the middle of the battlefield!

Is practicing His presence escapism? No, it is the maturity of one love, one goal, one unity of life. It's the perspective of the long-range view. It's seeing everything from the vantage point of the purposes of a good God.

Jesus said, "Do not let your hearts be troubled" (JOHN 14:1,27); in other words, "Don't allow it; it's bad for you."

Hear it again: *See everything from the vantage point of the purposes of a good God.*

> *Since, then, you have been raised with Christ,*
> *set your hearts on things above, where Christ*
> *is seated at the right hand of God. Set your*
> *minds on things above, not on earthly things*
> (COLOSSIANS 3:1,2).

Hear it once more: *See everything from the vantage point of the purposes of a good God.* When you do, your mind will be steadfastly at peace (ISAIAH 26:3), and you will have no fear of bad news (PSALM 112:7).

In the midst of all this writhing world, for believers God's presence is enough. He is—

> *A shelter from the wind,*
> *A refuge from the storm,*
>> *like streams of water in the desert*
>> *and the shadow of a great rock*
>>> *in a thirsty land* (ISAIAH 32:2).

He says His presence is your secured place (a well-stocked, fully protected bomb shelter!) until His wrath passes by (ISAIAH 26:20; 1 THESSALONIANS 5:9).

The God-designed ark in which Noah was temporarily housed had only one window: skyward. God tenderly shielded from Noah's sight all the surrounding struggling and death which was God's own judgment for rebellion and sin. Until it was over, Noah's only view was up.

See everything from the vantage point of the purposes of a good God.

14

How Important Is This Truth—to God and You?

In a Russian prison some years ago, 30 men of a non-Russian Orthodox church were being held and were brought before a judge. Their names were taken, 30 of them; they were carefully counted. As the officer finished the counting and started to leave, one prisoner spoke up.

"There's one name here you don't have," he said.

"No," was the answer; "I have all 30." And he counted them again.

"There's one more," insisted the prisoner. "You missed a name."

"Who?" demanded the official.

"The Lord Jesus," so the story goes.

And of course, Christ was just being His consistent self. Centuries earlier the apostle Paul had reported that at his trial "the Lord stood at my side and gave me strength" (2 TIMOTHY 4:17). And centuries before that, on the edge of a "vast and dreadful desert" across which the Israelites must travel (DEUTERONOMY 8:15),

God had assured Moses, "My Presence will go with you" (EXODUS 33:14).

And He will be with you too!

> When through the deep waters I call thee to go,
>   The rivers of sorrow shall not overflow;
> For I will be with thee, thy troubles to bless
>   And sanctify to thee thy deepest distress.[1]

There are some truths that are Mount Everests—snowcapped giants that rise up, up, up into the silences and mysteries that set them apart from other truths. Such a one is the truth that God has purposed in His heart to come down and live with His creation, His own dear people.

Even after His daily strollings in the Garden with them was cut off because of their sins, His plans moved forward to get rid of sin and death and at last live with them permanently. It was the reason for His tabernacle:

> *Have them make a sanctuary for me, and I will dwell among them* (EXODUS 25:8).

That sanctuary was just a "shadow," a "pattern," of the permanent one which will finally come. And one day when God has indeed destroyed all sin and death, then at last the new Jerusalem will descend from heaven, and a loud voice from the throne will make the official and final announcement:

> *Now the dwelling of God is with men, and he will live*
> *with them. They will be his people, and God himself*
> *will be with them and be their God* (REVELATION 21:3).

Oh, what a great day for the heart of God!

But all this is only the story of God's dwelling *with* His
people. Through the death and resurrection of His Son, the
Lord Jesus Christ, God forged an even greater intimacy—a
closeness never dreamed of before, not even by His most
saintly saints.

He would come more than "with," but actually *in.*

And for this—of such massive new importance—
one Person of the Godhead wouldn't do; two wouldn't
do; according to His incredible "mystery" and design
(EPHESIANS 3:4, 11), the divine Tri-unity, every part
of God, all of God, would come into the life and
even the body of the believer in Jesus Christ, to live
forever.

"Well," we say, "we know that the three are, after all,
one God." And MATTHEW 28:19 confirms this.

But how many functions of the Godhead do you see all
three Persons carrying out together? Not many. They are one
God, but usually their functions are separate.

The Father isn't the Son. The Spirit isn't the Father.
Although Jesus said that He and His Father are one (JOHN
10:30), more often He referred to their distinctivenesses.
When He was on earth He spoke of "my Father in
heaven" (MATTHEW 18:10). He said His Father loved Him

(JOHN 5:20) and had sent Him (JOHN 6:44), and that He would return to the Father (JOHN 13:1).

The Father made the same separation in His announcement out of heaven at Jesus' baptism (LUKE 3:22).

Only the Son was born that first Christmas day. Only the Son died on the cross—even temporarily forsaken by His Father (MATTHEW 27:46).

And the Holy Spirit, though within the Trinity one with the Father and the Son, has His own separate functions. At Pentecost it was the Spirit who filled the believers (ACTS 2:4).

Jesus Himself at one point separated all three Persons of the Trinity when He said:

> *The Counselor, the Holy Spirit, whom the Father will send in my name, will teach you all things and will remind you of everything I have said to you* (JOHN 14:26).

But—here's the Mount Everest!—God is so eager for intimacy with you that *the entire Godhead comes to live with you and within you,* right where you are, right now.

Jesus said it would happen; note the "we":

> *If anyone loves me . . . we will come into him and make our home with him* (JOHN 14:23).

If you're a Christian, God the Father dwells in you:

> *If anyone acknowledges that Jesus is the Son of God, God lives in him and he in God* (1 JOHN 4:15).

(Who is as relational as God? He loves to love! He loves to fellowship! He loves to be close to His own!)

If you're a Christian, Jesus Christ dwells in you:

> *God has chosen to make known among the Gentiles the glorious riches of this mystery, which is Christ in you, the hope of glory* (COLOSSIANS 1:27).

If you're a Christian, the Holy Spirit dwells in you:

> *[God] . . . put his Spirit in our hearts as a deposit, guaranteeing what is to come* (2 CORINTHIANS 1:21, 22).

This means that the power of the Father Himself lives in you:

> *Now to him who is able to do immeasurably more than all we ask or imagine, according to his power that is at work within us, to him be glory* (EPHESIANS 3:20, 21).

It means that the knowledge of the love of Christ is in you:

> *. . . that Christ may dwell in your hearts through faith . . . that you . . . may have power . . . to grasp how wide and long and high and deep is the love of Christ, and to know this love that surpasses knowledge— that you may be filled to the measure of all the fullness of God* (EPHESIANS 3:17–19)!

And it means that the gift of the Holy Spirit is in you:

> We know that we live in him and he in us, because he
> has given us of his Spirit (1 JOHN 4:13).

And—

> The fruit of the Spirit is love, joy, peace, patience, kind-
> ness, goodness, faithfulness, gentleness, and self-control
> (GALATIANS 5:22, 23).

All this has been given to you!

Then obey His command to be filled full to overflow-
ing with His Spirit (EPHESIANS 5:18), so that all His charac-
teristics may be yours in abundance.

And offer God the Trinity all the worship of your heart,
for you have been totally invaded by Him.

> Let all mortal flesh keep silence
>   And with fear and trembling stand;
> Ponder nothing earthly minded,
>   For with blessing in His hand
> [All] our God to earth descendeth,
>   Our full homage to demand.[2]

There have been times when the two of us have had to
absolutely cling to the presence of the powerful, triune God.
When the crises came, we needed all of Him!

Ray: One of the desperate times in our life together
came when we had to know whether or not we were

to leave pastoring Lake Avenue Congregational Church in Pasadena, California.

We had been there 20 years—from age 35 to 55. That's a long time, a big chunk of our lives. Our children had gone from ages 12, 11, and 10 to 32, 31, and 30, with an added one now age 14. The dear congregation had celebrated with us three weddings, the adoption of a new baby, and the births of eight grandchildren. And we had been through all the joys and griefs of our people, grown in number from 1700 to 3300. How precious they were to us! The marriage of pastor and people was a good marriage.

Then there were the 12 full-time pastors on staff, the finest combination of skills and godliness I have ever seen. How we loved each other! I knew that my leaving would disrupt 12 strategic careers.

Still, I was out of gas. Much as I loved the people and staff and knew they loved me, I was at the end of my strength. I came back each Tuesday after Mondays off, still tired. I came back each September after Augusts off, still tired. My hands were starting to shake. My ears were starting to ring.

Anne and I sought the Lord together. I wouldn't have budged an inch unless we were in full agreement, and so far we weren't.

We were flying to Alaska to do some speaking when suddenly she turned to me in the plane and said, "Ray, I think you should go. I believe it's the right thing to do."

Suddenly after that God was speaking through everybody! A minister in London said to me, "Ray, don't stay in your pastorate too long. I did: My people and I loved each other so much that I missed the warning signals. But I had gotten too familiar to them. I had become to them like part of the woodwork. They loved me, but they weren't listening."

God's final shove came on a Sunday morning when Lake Avenue had a guest preacher. This freed me to slip out of each of the three morning services for a while to observe the Sunday school.

As I poked my head in the back door of one of the large adult classes the teacher, one of my very dear friends, was saying, "When you know what God is telling you to do, move! Don't vacillate! Don't argue, don't dillydally, *move!*" (Later when I told him the implication of his words, Bill was shocked.)

I backed out of the door saying, "Lord, I hear You. Father, Son, Holy Spirit, You have spoken to me. I have no idea where I'm going, but I dare not disobey. My tenure here at Lake Avenue is over."

In two months I was gone, and I've never looked back. It was right for the church, and it was right for me. In their two wonderful pastorates since, then they have built their gorgeous 4500-seat sanctuary and they're moving ahead. And as much as I will always love them, God has faithfully blessed Anne and me in these subsequent years of writing, radio, and speaking.

Oh, the blessedness of knowing that all of God is with all of us—always!

> *Those who know your name will trust in you,*
> *for you, Lord, have never forsaken those who seek*
> *you* (PSALM 9:10).

Praise to the Trinity! Praise for His awesome God-ness; praise for His breathtaking closeness—to us, to you!

> God is over all things,
> under all things,
> outside all;
> within but not enclosed;
> without but not excluded;
> above but not raised up;
> below but not depressed;
> wholly above, presiding;
> wholly beneath, sustaining;
> wholly within, filling.[3]

Give yourself completely to Him, because He gives Himself completely to you.

The Experience
of
His Presence

The king said to me, "What is it you
want?" Then I prayed to the God of
heaven, and I answered the king. . . .
—NEHEMIAH 2:4,5

15

A Longing for His Presence

We said we've never had any ecstatic experiences, but we've certainly known times when God's presence was very real.

A while back we were concluding a conference with missionaries on the island of Saipan. We hadn't seen outright revival in our conferences for a good while, though we had been working as hard as ever.

During the final meeting we were both very tired. But the response of those missionaries became the thing which we aim for and pray for—something that only God, coming sovereignly in His presence and His power, can accomplish. Relationships were healed within a few hours that might otherwise have taken years. The missionaries freely opened their hearts to each other; there was brokenness, honesty, repentance, affirmations, and expressions of encouragement and love; there was much laughter and many tears.

We might say, to be dramatic, "God came!" No, God is always with His people—that's His promise. But even as Jesus, though always Deity, chose a special moment on a mountaintop to reveal His Deity's glory, so at special times God chooses to make His presence among His people especially real and powerful.

In the middle of that gathering on Saipan, the two of us caught each other's eyes, and through our tears we grinned. Along with the others, we were exhilarated; fatigue was gone.

The practice of His presence really means deciding to believe that He is with you whether you sense it or not. It's a commitment you make. You acknowledge that *He is with you*—now and every moment from now on.

Then probably, sooner or later, *believing* will become *seeing*. After your commitment may follow the experiences, the emotions, the new revelations of understanding. You don't demand them, but you long for them.

To feel His presence, to meet our God in special times and ways, to experience the overshadowing of His Holy Spirit in power—this has been the desire of God's people through the years.

"One thing I ask of the Lord," wrote David—only one thing! May the Spirit give you, and us too, such single hearts.

> *One thing I ask of the Lord,*
> *this is what I seek:*
> *that I may dwell in the house of the Lord*
> *all the days of my life [not just today],*
> *to gaze upon the beauty of the Lord*
> *and to seek him in his temple* (PSALM 27:4).

Now David was only the king, and no king—no one but priests—was ever allowed to set foot inside God's temple. King Uzziah later tried it, and God instantly and permanently struck him with leprosy (2 CHRONICLES 26:16–21).

So what did David mean, that he yearned to dwell all his life in the house of the Lord? He meant the same thing we would mean: to abide in the sweetness and power of His presence, to dwell with Him in joy continually even while doing his earthly duties, to seek His face constantly and to spiritually gaze upon Him, feeling Him close.

All the psalms become even more precious when we interpret references to God's house, tent, courts, and temple in this way:

> *I long to dwell in your tent forever*
> > *and take refuge in the shelter of your wings*
> > (PSALM 61:4).

> *Surely goodness and love will follow me*
> > *all the days of my life,*
> *And I will dwell in the house of the Lord*
> > *forever* (PSALM 23:6).

> *I have seen you in the sanctuary*
> > *and beheld your power and your glory* (PSALM 63:2).

> *Lord, who may dwell in your sanctuary?* . . .
> > *[not literal descendants of Levi, qualified by being*
> > *born into the line of priests]—*

> *He whose walk is blameless* (PSALM 15:1,2).
> *He who has clean hands and a pure heart* (PSALM 24:4).

This insight makes PSALM 84 even stronger. It was written by the sons of Korah, who were Kohathites—priests—and who spent their whole adult lives ministering in God's temple. And yet look at verses 2, 4, and 10:

> *My soul yearns, even faints,*
> > *for the courts of the Lord;*
> *my heart and my flesh cry out*
> > *for the living God. . . .*
> *Blessed are those who dwell in your house;*
> > *they are ever praising you. . . .*
> *Better is one day in your courts*
> > *than a thousand elsewhere. . . .*

In other words, "Lord, I'm in church all the time; but I'm not satisfied to be merely serving inside four walls. I long for Your very presence, joining those blessed ones [verse 4] who dwell there continually and whose hearts are constantly praising You. That's what I want!"

Oh, may your heart also cry, "Open the gates of the temple!" to strengthen you in the stresses of daily living and to give you tastes of eternity to come.

> *Ray:* I was preaching my heart out once, in the days when I was pastor of Lake Avenue Congregational Church, and my "zeal consumed me." In the heat of the moment I cried, "Look, friends—here at this church we want nothing less than to go hard after

God. If you don't want to join us in this, just go find another church somewhere!"

I finished the sermon and we were singing a closing hymn, and the presence of God invaded me in a special way. Suddenly I knew I'd been crude, I'd been rough with those dear people. In that moment I was rebuked and reminded that "the Spirit of the Lord does not strive."

I stopped the hymn we were singing, and I apologized then and there to the people. I know it was a tender moment, and that God used my sin and my repentance to bring us closer together than we would otherwise have been.

Friend, look for, long for, pray for, and expect special breaking-through times when God makes His presence very real, very powerful! And until they come, dwell in His presence by faith and gaze upon His beauty.

16

Elliot, Cushman, Us

"I walked out to the hill just now," wrote Jim Elliot in his diary. "It is exalting, delicious. To stand embraced by the shadows of a friendly tree with the wind tugging at your coat-tail and the heavens hailing your heart—to gaze and glory and give oneself again to God, what more could a man ask? Oh, the fullness, pleasure, sheer excitement of knowing God on earth!"[1]

Jim Elliot, like Enoch (GENESIS 5:24), "walked with God; then he was no more, because God took him away." Not long after this entry in his diary, Jim, an American missionary serving in Ecuadorean jungles, was martyred. But the truth of his experience goes on, alive and well.

Ralph Cushman tells about a man blinded in his late twenties in an industrial accident, who 30 years later suddenly could see again. His exhilaration in rediscovering the world sounds remarkably like the exhilaration that others experience when they discover the presence of God:

Sitting in my big armchair last Monday night, I suddenly seemed to see a curtain rise. Not wishing to frighten my wife, who was reading to me, I said, very calmly, "Something has happened. I believe I can see."

Then I was sure that I saw the sofa with a blue pillow and a gold, and then I saw a strange kindly-faced woman whom I did not know. "What is it?" said the woman, and then I knew it was my wife. She started to cry. "Don't cry," I said. "Laugh and be happy!" She almost fell, and I caught her and helped her back to her chair.

Now, after four days of sight, the world is beginning to take on proportions again. . . . Everything is so changed that I must touch the objects around me to believe my eyes. . . . I am very happy but I can scarcely sleep nights for thinking about it. Yesterday I saw flowers for the first time in thirty years and hung around them like a bee.[2]

Dr. Cushman tells how as a boy he heard an older Christian say that he was conscious of Christ's presence beside him as he walked. Cushman the boy asked himself, "I wonder if he really meant what he said, or was he just using a figure of speech?"

Later on [he writes], someone gave me Phillips Brooks' words: "It is no figure of speech. . . . He is here. I know Him. He knows me. It is the realest thing in the world, and every day it grows realer."

These words are worth repeating over and over
again; they have come to be very precious to me.
And so, too, has grown to be the experience of the
Presence![3]

The two of us don't want just to quote others' experiences but tell you our own.

After that life-changing August when reading Brother
Lawrence started us on our new adventure, we have taught
the concept of "practicing the presence of God" to hundreds
of people, with great delight to our hearts. Over and over
we've said, "The knowledge of God's presence will cheer you.
But the practice of His presence will revolutionize you."

Some of our speaking notes go like this:

One of the central truths of the Bible. Not men-
tioned much in theology, but spread across the pages
of Old Testament, New Testament. . . .

PSALM 16:8–11: prophetic psalm but also David's
own experience:

"I have set [or fixed] the Lord always before me.
Because he is at my right hand [in Scriptures, symbol
of presence] I will not be shaken."

(Lots of shook-up Christians these days!)

Verse 9: "Therefore my heart is glad" (when He's
fixed always before you your disposition will show it)

Verse 9: "And my tongue rejoices" (your conversation will reveal it)

Verse 9: "My body also will rest secure" (can even make a difference in your physical well-being). . . .

PROVERBS 3:6: "In all your ways" (running, working at desk, cleaning house, driving car) "acknowledge Him. . . ."

We have taught this and much more, with blessing to ourselves and others.

But the last few months, working on this book—! What can we say? In our consciousness He is much closer. We have both remarked about it. John Owen's comment about the Lord's being "silent because of His love" was new to us and permeated us deeply. "Lord, You really, really love us! . . . Lord, You're really, really here, closer than close! . . ." It has enlivened our consciousness of personal sin and renewed our longing to be holy.

Helen Keller, who could neither see nor hear, expressed that God's presence felt to her like a "warmth."

Certainly for us it is comforting and happy. We know that He delights in us, and we delight in Him. It renews in us a certain "fear of the Lord," that in these last decades of our life we don't want to "blow it" but be faithful unto death.

We notice we're talking about the Lord together more than ever, being more continually conscious of Him. To tell you the truth, we laugh together more and kiss and hug more than we ever have. Our fellowship together has never been closer or sweeter, as our fellowship with Him becomes the same.

Surely in God's presence PROVERBS 4:18 is true:

> *The path of the righteous is like the first gleam of dawn,*
> *shining ever brighter till the full light of day!*

17

❦

Excerpts from Anne's Daily Written Prayers

"**H**ow wonderful, Lord: We don't need to compete for Your blessings, to beat out others to get to You first. 'Not to the swift is the race.' You reach to the slowest, the weakest, the poorest.

"Lord, I am slow, I am weak, I am poor. I come to You for mercy, and I find that You have already come to me! You have made the cross a bridge to me, and You are here, with me, and I am loved and accepted. Praise, praise, praise! . . .

"O Lord of heaven and Lord over all, You have ordained the people in my life who witness of You to me. Thank You for Bible characters, for history's great souls, for my parents, for Ray, for . . . others—Lord, in the light of them I want to throw off all hindrances and the sins that are so ready to trip me up, and run with grace and patience and sweetness of attitude the race that You have marked out just for me.

"Lord, You are my righteousness! Without You there would be nothing commendable in my life at all. But because Christ is in me and the Holy Spirit infills me and You are my help, I want to fix my eyes on You and consider You, study You, focus on You, examine You, emulate You as long as I live. I know this will enable me not to grow weary and lose heart (HEBREWS 12:3). Your almighty power has given me all I need for life and godliness (2 PETER 1:3).

"O Lord God! What a wonder You are! How strong, how beautiful, how attractive, how full of splendor and radiance, how awesome in Your power, how perfectly balanced in Your justice, how wise—knowing the end from the beginning—how noble, drawing Your people ever upward, ever upward, how gracious and longsuffering—full of lovingkindness and tender mercies and compassion!

"Dear Father! In the light of You I fall flat. There is nothing worthy in me; in the light of all Your glorious attributes I fall short, I miss the mark, I am an altogether unprofitable servant, even my righteousness is as filthy rags. Not unto us, Lord, not unto us be the glory. Father, I am embarrassed and humiliated; my sins of omission condemn me as much as my sins of commission.

"And yet You love me, You love me, You really, really totally love me! You accept me! You take me from the miry pit and make me altogether righteous like Your Son! O my Abba Father, I draw close, and I say thank You, thank You, thank You! Holy Spirit, fill me with more gratitude than I have yet known, for all that You are and all that You have done for me. Alleluia! Alleluia! Alleluia!"

18

The Experience of His Presence

Anne: Let's go back once more to just after that first Brother-Lawrence August—to a few weeks later, when Ray preached for the first time about practicing the presence of God to our Pasadena congregation. The people were aware that for Ray it was preaching new truth. They sat very still . . . They always did, but there was something in the atmosphere which said it was particularly sit-up-and-pay-attention time.

After church I was headed for my Sunday school class on the top floor of one of the education buildings, and a certain fellow waited with me at the elevator. I knew him; he was the manager of a local hamburger place. His eyes were glowing.

"Anne," said my friend, "from now on, God and I are going to cook hamburgers together." It was heartwarming in the months that followed to hear how many "burger" people came to know Jesus!

I know that for myself, I went home from
church that day hardly able to contain myself until I
could get through dinner and put a song onto paper:

> Lord, You're here! I bow in Your presence.
> Long have You said You'd forever abide,
> And long I assented, but dull and unheeding,
> Without an awareness of You at my side.

Lord, You're here! Make me aware!
Lord, You're here! Keep me rememb'ring!
Lord, You're here! Open my eyes, open my eyes. . . .

> Lord, You're here! I'll truly believe it.
> Off with my shoes as I bow in this spot;
> Like Jacob, exclaiming, "How holy this place is!
> The Lord has been present, and I knew it not. . . ."

Lord, You're here! You're not just a doctrine,
A concept to use or discard like a toy,
But You, Lord, Yourself, in Your very own Person,
And oh! how Your presence brings fullness of joy!

> Lord, You're here! Make me aware!
> Lord, You're here! Keep me rememb'ring!
> Lord, You're here! Open my eyes,
> Open my eyes, open my eyes![1]

When God chooses to let His presence be brilliantly
manifest, what a lifting, what an encouraging, what a time

of glory for His people! Early in American history David Brainard, missionary to the Indians, wrote in his diary about this kind of experience:

> After I rode more than two miles, it came to my mind to dedicate myself to God again, which I did with great solemnity and unspeakable satisfaction. Especially I gave up myself to Him renewedly in the work of the ministry . . . without any exception or reserve. . . .
>
> I seemed to be most free, cheerful, and full in this dedication of myself. . . . My whole soul cried, "Lord, to Thee I dedicate myself! . . . Lord, I desire nothing else; I desire nothing more. . . . Whom have I in heaven but Thee? And there is none upon earth that I desire besides Thee."[2]

Think about Job. He had cried out:

> *If I only knew where to find him;*
> *if only I could go to his dwelling! . . .*
> *But if I go to the east, he is not there;*
> *if I go to the west, I do not find him* (JOB 23:3, 8).

That's the most basic reason—not his circumstances— why Job was depressed and miserable. True living is always "between our ears."

But God graciously revealed Himself to Job, and Job's words at the end are these:

> *My ears had heard of you*
>> *but now my eyes have seen you* (JOB 42:5).

Moffatt's version says:

> *I had heard of Thee by hearsay,*
>> *but now mine eyes have seen Thee!*

No more secondhand faith for Job; now His relationship with Almighty God was actually personal. Now he had convictions about God not because he had been an elder in his church, so to speak, or the patriarch of his distinguished family, or a leader in worship. . . . No, being all of those things, he had still been totally despairing. But then the presence of God invaded his life.

Really, Job didn't find God; *God found Job.* God understood when Job had suffered enough to get all the self-righteousness out of him; and then, says JOB 38:1,

> *The Lord answered Job* out of the storm.

Says Oswald Chambers:

> First God gives us a vision; then he takes us down into the valley and batters us into the shape of the vision. And it is in the valley that so many of us faint and give way.[3]

But if your eyes are steadfastly fixed on Him, Christian, then *even in the battering* you know that Christ is in you, on you, with you, beside you, underneath you, above you. His love is your love, His joy is your joy, His rest is your rest, His life is your life. You are in Him, and He is in you. He takes all your burdens and griefs; you take all His peace and power. It's the exchanged life.

And so, eventually, the agony is replaced by ecstasy.

19

The Fellowship of His Presence

God has invaded you, believer, with His presence; and it is thrilling to discover others who also know they're invaded. God-enthralled people soon discover others who are God-enthralled; the network reaches out and forms a sweet union.

"Revival people" understand their fellowship together. They don't create it or decide it or organize it—they just discover it. And they know they're not in a democracy but in a theocracy, where Christ rules and directs and guides all together. And the center of authority isn't in the invaded ones but in the Beloved Invader, not in the created ones but in the Creator. He is the instigator; the energy flows from Him.

In Him we become one—an enormous one, larger than logical addition, a mystic body of extended unity in Christ. Jesus Himself reached out His arms and said, "He who is not against us is for us." What a lovely ingathering!

And yet He also said, "He who is not for us is against us." What do we see here—a surprising elitism?

Well, the invitation into an awareness of the presence of God is restricted. He is not there for everybody. One of the disciples asked Jesus, "Lord, why do you intend to show yourself to us and not to the world?" (JOHN 14:22).

Jesus' answer (JOHN 14:23, 24) sounds exclusive because it is! He says, "If anyone loves me [that's the qualifier] . . . my Father will love him, and we will come to him and make our home with him."

This is intimacy with God which millions know nothing about. There's a sign posted on the door: "Those who love Jesus only."

Jesus told His disciples:

> *Before long, the world will not see me anymore, but you will see me* (JOHN 14:19).

And indeed, following His resurrection this is what Peter reported:

> *He was not seen by all the people, but by witnesses whom God had already chosen—by us who ate and drank with him after he rose from the dead* (Acts 10:41).

And this fellowship continues to this day, as believers have "the eyes of their hearts" opened to Him (EPHESIANS 1:18).

It's a quiet, unheralded fellowship.

In JUDGES 7 Gideon was given command of an army of 32,000 with which to battle the Midianites, but God said, "You have too many men" (verse 2). What kind of military strategy was that?

So at God's command Gideon sent home all the soldiers who were afraid—22,000 of them. But God looked at the 10,000 left and said, "There are still too many" (verse 4).

Then God had Gideon take the men down to water, and told him in effect, "Send home all the fellows who kneel to drink; save back all who lap the water like a dog with their tongues." That left just 300 men, and with these 300 God gave a great victory over the Midianites!

What was the point? God explained it: "in order that Israel may not boast" (JUDGES 7:2).

If within the church of God there were a highly visible majority who crowed over their close fellowship with Him, what a carnal, competitive free-for-all that would make!

In the Corinthian church the carnal Christians were apparently the majority, and they were the loud ones, bragging about who followed what spiritual leader (1 CORINTHIANS 1:11,12). In the Galatian church the carnal Christians were apparently the majority, pushing a gospel of legalism. And in the days of Israelite degeneracy, the carnal priests were apparently the majority, bringing foreigners into the temple and desecrating the sanctuary (EZEKIEL 44:7,8).

But who was it among God's people that He had a special weakness for? It wasn't the many who ran the race, but the one who went into strict training and got

the prize (1 CORINTHIANS 9:24, 25). It wasn't the many
who followed legalizers (GALATIANS 5:10–12; 6:12,13), but
those who lived by the Spirit (GALATIANS 5:16, 22, 23).
And it wasn't the wishy-washy majority of Israelite priests,
but the descendants of Zadok who followed God without
compromise (EZEKIEL 44:10–16). The Levites, the majority,
had served the Israelite people; in fact, they were so eager
to please the people that they'd even assisted them in their
idol worship! So God said, "All right, from now on you
may no longer serve Me; all you can do is serve the
people":

> *Stand before the people and serve them. . . .*
> *But the . . . descendents of Zadok . . . who*
> *faithfully carried out the duties of my sanctuary*
> *when Israel went astray from me, are to come*
> *near to minister before me; they are to stand*
> *before me and . . . minister before me* (verses
> 11,15,16).

Have you noticed the difference between serving *people*
in all the busywork of Christendom and serving *the Lord
Himself?* God in heaven says He is endlessly wearied by all
the paper-shuffling and supper-serving and task-force-dis-
cussing which merely keeps organizational wheels turning.

> *Who has asked this of you,*
> *this trampling in my courts?*
> *Stop bringing meaningless offerings! . . .*
> *I cannot bear your evil assemblies.*

Your . . . festivals and your appointed feasts
  my soul hates.
They have become a burden to me;
  I am weary of bearing them.
When you spread out your hands in prayer
  I will hide my eyes from you (ISAIAH 1:12–15).

When our Christianity turns horizontal—when we begin merely to serve people—eventually everyone gets carnal and exhausted.

When we minister to the Lord Himself, He and we enjoy mutual delight.

Serve the Lord with gladness;
  come before His presence with singing . . . .
Enter into His gates with thanksgiving,
  and into His courts with praise (PSALM 100:2,4 NKJV).

The Lord delights in those who fear him,
  who put their hope in his unfailing love
  (PSALM 147:11).

This what the Lord says: . . .
  "Let him who boasts boast about this:
  that he understands and knows me . . .
  for in these I delight"(JEREMIAH 9:23,24).

Come along, Christian, with that exhilarated, exhilarating crowd—similar to the ones who used to go up annually to Jerusalem, the great city which personified the very presence of God. With excitement and anticipation they sang all the "songs of ascents," PSALMS 120 to 134, as they journeyed. They traveled "up," and their songs and moods were also "up."

> *I rejoiced with those who said to me,*
> *"Let us go to the house of the Lord"* (PSALM 122:1).

Oh, the thrill! In lockstep with fellow-travelers, Christian, we're marching from grace to glory.

20

The Benefit of His Presence

Ray: There was a time when God gave me a special
period during which He wanted me to lean hard on
His presence.

I'd had a routine physical checkup, and the
nurse phoned to say that one finding was irregular
and I needed to make another appointment with the
doctor right away. She'd said enough, but in a weak
moment the nurse went on to remark that the finding showed I had cancer.

This was on a late Monday afternoon. I was
leaving early Tuesday morning for Los Angeles for
three straight days of broadcasting; there was no way
I could get back to the doctor until late Thursday afternoon.

For three long days Anne and I lived with the
nurse's report—in a lovely sense of calm and peace.

"Why should we feel we're exempt from
human miseries?" we asked each other. "Actually,
we're long overdue . . . ."

"God has always been good to us. He is good to us now with this news, and He will be nothing but good to us through all the experiences to come . . ."

"As Job said, 'Shall we accept good from God and not trouble?' . . ."

"We trust Him. . . . We love God. . . . We will love Him through this. . . . We trust Him. . . ."

So we talked to each other by phone in the in-between moments.

On Thursday we walked into the doctor's office together to hear our news, and he was surprised at the nurse's comment. "Cancer? There's very little chance of that. We'll do further testing, but the possibility is remote. . . ." But we praised God for all the peace He'd given us during those three days.

On Friday Anne flew to Kansas City to speak at a weekend women's conference. That evening a Nebraska farmer's wife came to her to report a recent experience.

She said, "This past week I listened each morning to the *Haven of Rest* broadcast on our little kitchen radio, and my husband listened in the barn, as the two of us always do. Yesterday—Thursday— he happened to say to me, 'Isn't it a shame that Ray Ortlund has cancer!'

"I was shocked. I said, 'Ray Ortlund doesn't have cancer!'

" 'Yes, he does,' my husband said. 'He talked about it on the Monday broadcast.'

"Now, I happened to remember," this farmer's wife told Anne, "that on Monday Ray had read a letter on the air from somebody who wrote 'I have cancer . . .' and I said to my husband, 'Did you turn on your radio a little late?'

" 'As a matter of fact, I did,' my husband said.

" 'Well, he didn't say *he* had cancer; he was reading a letter from someone who said 'I have cancer.'

"We both felt relieved to have the thing settled, but my husband said, 'For the last three days I've prayed so hard for Ray and Anne! I prayed two things—that God would save Ray's health and that He would give both of them absolute calm and peace.' "

When the young wife said that, Anne was amazed. "Monday to Thursday were exactly the three days that we thought Ray *did* have cancer!" Anne said, and she told our side of the story.

Then Anne told her, "God absolutely answered your husband's prayers for us. He was undoubtedly the only person in the world interceding for us those three days in those two specific ways. God *did* preserve Ray's health, and He did indeed give us calm and peace through the whole experience."

"In the shelter of your presence you hide them," sings David to God in PSALM 31:20.

Yes, He does hide His people. He covers them with His feathers, and under His wings they find refuge (PSALM 91:4). *He is with them.*

As Jesus left this earth in His resurrection body, it's the thing He saved to say last:

> *Surely I am with you always, to the very end of the age* (MATTHEW 28:20).

As He was about to leave them (seemingly), what could have been more reassuring?

And just as He would be with the apostles, to make sense out of what to them would otherwise have been unthinkable—Jesus permanently removed in body—so He was with the two of us those three days, and so He is with you.

Sometimes your path may seem suddenly dark. Listen—the light of His presence is always enough to give you insight to go on. *He is with you*, to put a ramrod down your spine so that in the treacherous places you can hang tough.

He is with you always; the Greek says "all the days," every single day—first Sunday, then Monday, then Tuesday—day after day after day.

Even in His newly resurrected body Jesus "appeared to them over a period of forty days" (ACTS 1:3) only intermittently.

But no more! With His ascension into heaven He promised a new, greatly expanded Presence—being everywhere, at every time, with every believer, "to the very end of the age."

The promise of His perpetual presence. . . .

Through the hard times, what a promise!

21

The Spirit's Schooling Versus Your Own Schooling

Don't try to "train" yourself to be in His presence; He is here. Just acknowledge it and start living in the light of it.

Many Christians stumble here; they think that somehow their own determination and self-control will bring Him close. No, He *is* close. But let His lovingkindness and patience with you draw you to apologize for your delay, and then start enjoying Him.

There's no secret technique to "do it," to practice His presence. There are no six ways to become at home with Him, no ten steps of technique to get it right—no formula at all.

Just be drawn by His love into an awareness of what already is. Then you'll be guided and stimulated by the deep impressions of your heart.

Those who are led by the Spirit of God are sons of God (ROMANS 8:14).

You can trust His directing; don't worry—He won't lead you astray. And your loving compliance with His direction will be the very proof that you're truly His.

Don't feel you must always verbalize to Him. We two are happy just to enjoy each other's presence sometimes without comment. To be in one another's loving company is enough. So with God.

Gradually a "Presence-attitude" will develop in your heart. The undercurrent of His nearness will be a great comfort. In outwardly stormy times you'll glance at Him inwardly and smile. Behind the foreground of circumstances will be the background of God's loveliness and power.

You will go through times when your soul's heart is dull. You will feel a distance between you and God; shrug it off—it's not reality, only your faulty perception of reality, and it will pass. Walk with Him anyhow; talk with Him anyhow; tell Him the distance you're feeling, but don't be gloomy about it. Let the habit of your worship go right on.

We sensuous people of current times want everything to relate to our bodies. They're too important to us! When we think of practicing the presence of God we want to see and hear, involving our bodies to the neglect of our spirits. Like the immature Christians of COLOSSIANS 2:21, we're too concerned with handling, tasting, touching. We want visions and voices; we complain that God isn't "real" to us. . . . The New-Testament-age Jews, unwilling to give up

their religion of temples and lambs, "required a sign"—
something tangible.

Oh, listen! Be thankful if the jolts and tingles come, but
be deeply satisfied with the theology, the knowledge, of His
presence! Investigate in His Word the truth of it until that
truth overwhelms you and excites you—without any feeling, seeing, hearing, or touching at all!

Pray "that Christ may dwell in your hearts *through
faith*" (EPHESIANS 3:17); it is *through faith* that you will get
"rooted and established."

How can we absolutely count on God making Himself
real to us? "The Spirit himself testifies with our spirit," says
ROMANS 8:16.

How can we "see"? "The eyes of our hearts [are] being
enlightened," says EPHESIANS 1:18.

> *Anne:* I remember once a girl phoned me who I knew
> had been in depression for about a month. She said,
> "Anne, I just had to call you and tell you what I just
> read in C.S. Lewis.
>
> "He said, when you feel like praising God and
> you praise Him, that's wonderful. But if you don't
> feel like praising Him and you praise Him anyway,
> that's an exceptionally sweet fragrance in His nos-
> trils. So right now I've been praising Him."
>
> And the tone of her voice was more lifted than
> I had heard from her in a long time.

22

✦━✦

Starting Out

When you begin to discover God's presence in your life, don't make the mistake of thinking that God has just walked in on you, and that this is some brand-new thing.

He has always been there in your life, since before the foundation of the world—loving you, making plans for you, caring for you (PSALM 139:15,16). You don't make Him present; He has been there forever.

Think of it as coming into a meeting late. The action doesn't begin with you, your entrance, your experience; it's been going on a long time. Slip into His presence quietly, humbly. Ask forgiveness for your tardiness. Learn what's been going on; seek to catch up. What has He been up to? Consider EPHESIANS 1:4; ROMANS 8:29,30; EPHESIANS 2:10.

"Christ in you," says Paul. He is there in your inner secret places, influencing you, urging you as you respond to His gentle pressures. He is there in great power: He, the Instructor, you, the learner (pay attention!). But He's also there for fellowship and joy.

In shady green pastures so rich and so sweet
God leads His dear children along.

How do you live in Christ? How do you enjoy His presence more? By turning to Him in continual prayer and worship, whatever else you're doing. By constantly surrendering, surrendering to Him, as you see His will through the day. By saying, "Yes, Lord. . . . I love You, Lord. . . ."

Whatever your lapses and failures, quickly repent and get back again to the reality of that quiet recognition of God. It's a schooling, with grade levels.

> *Blessed are those who have* learned *to acclaim you,*
> *who walk in the light of your presence, O Lord.*
> *They rejoice in your name all day long;*
> *they exult in your righteousness.*
> *For you are their glory and strength* (PSALM 89:15–17).

God's presence will make you a happy person!

There's a door standing open in heaven, and the Lord is saying, "Come up here" (REVELATION 4:1). Even right now as you read, offer yourself to Christ. Surrender to Him; begin to live with Christ as you live with your family, your friends, your work. It takes discipline, bringing your thoughts into captivity, but it isn't "psyching yourself up." It's living with reality; God Himself is your constant reality.

Walking, driving, talking, listening, eating, working— you're with Him, behind the scenes in simple prayer. He is there when you fall asleep. He is there when you wake up. Brother Lawrence says, "Those who have at their backs the gale of the Holy Spirit go forward even in sleep!"

You may feel awkward, but go on. Don't choose to live in the presence of your problems, your lacks, your needs, your irritations, your frustrations; choose instead to point your heart in the direction of Christ. All day long solve challenges in Christ, work out problems in Christ, be aware of Him, and ask His help as you do what you do. Do it all in Christ!

Both your inner life and outer life are already absolutely open to Him.

> *Jesus knew in his spirit that this was what they were thinking in their hearts* (MARK 2:8).

> *He did not need man's testimony about man, for he knew what was in a man* (JOHN 2:25).

"Everything is [already] uncovered and laid bare before the eyes of him to whom we must give an account" (HEBREWS 4:13).

So "walk and talk with Him, as good friends should and do."

Your practicing the presence of God will result in a gradual but drastic redirecting of your life, a massive revision of your thinking, feeling, and acting. God will loosen the chains that bind you to your former ways. He will release you from your rights, your demands—all that part of you that has kept you tense and frustrated.

> *You will keep in perfect peace*
> *   him whose mind is steadfast,*
> *   because he trusts in you. . . .*

The path of the righteous is level;
O upright One, you make the way
of the righteous smooth.
Yes, Lord, walking in the way of your laws,
we wait for you;
your name and renown
are the desire of our hearts (ISAIAH 26:3, 7, 8).

Your accomplishments will multiply because of new freedom and energizing and efficiency in the Spirit; but then you will realize,

Lord...all that we have accomplished
you have done for us (ISAIAH 26:12).

Henry Jowett tells of hearing Professor Henry Drummond speak to his university students like this:

Men, do you mean business? Is your religion to be a business or a toy? If you're going to play with it, drop it. If you mean business, put out your hand and grasp God's, and then mean business all your life.[1]

When you go after a moment-by-moment awareness of the immediacy of God, you're not going after marginal concerns but the deepest stuff of life. You'll have a sense of removal from all that's "below"—from self-deceptions, fads, culturized Christianity. You'll renounce the superficial, the trite, the trendy in favor of the genuine, the fruitful, the "above." Your ear will quit listening to "Thus saith the majority" and hear instead "Thus saith the Lord."

This kind of living should actually be for all believers the most normal. It's the restful, happy, holy, loving way to live.

And now, will you accept it? You're facing one of the great decisions of your life. Forgive us if we quote the words of one of our former books:

> How patient God is! Think how many times He has flashed lightning across the sky. Through the ages it would splinter huge trees. It would run a cow down a path, while people watched and wondered. All the time God was trying to tell them something.
>
> One stormy day a man finally went out with a kite and a key. All heaven was probably bending over saying, "All these years we've been trying to tell them about electricity. Look, look, he's got it: at last, he's got it!" And soon the world lit up.
>
> How long, how long you and we have been vaguely aware—theoretically aware—of God's presence with us! What do you think: has all heaven been waiting and perhaps saying, "I think they might get it. I think at last they're starting to get it!"[2]

Christian, you may have been saved one, ten, or forty years. But maybe at last you're going to get it! You can't get more of Christ than you've had, but you can learn to recognize Him in a new way and enjoy a new relationship with Him.

Live your Christian life from the inside to the outside; it's very simple. At the center is God the Father, Son, and Holy Spirit and all His glory. Live with Him there.

Have you got it?

A One-Week Experiment

My Presence will go with you,
and I will give you rest.
—Exodus 33:14

23

Introduction to the Week

However long it has taken you to read to this point in our book, stop for now. The following pages are to be read during your coming week, one section each day. If you "mean business," as Professor Drummond said, ask God this coming week to move you in the direction of starting to live continually in His presence. Each day's reading is to stimulate you toward that end.

This week for us was Thanksgiving, and at our house we alternate homes each year among the family members and share a potluck meal. (We do that for Christmas and birthdays, too.) Of course this week it was turkey, stuffing, mashed potatoes and gravy, candied sweet potatoes, squash with fruit, green beans, jellied salad, rolls, and several kinds of pies.

Usually by the end of the main course we're too stuffed to go on, and we take a family hike around the block. Or move on to somebody else's house while everything's settling down inside us.

That's what you need to do at this point in your reading: Take a break! Consider your week starting tomorrow as your "walk around the block." It's essential not only to eat but to *exercise*—not only to read truth but to *do* it.

Ask God the Father, Son, and Holy Spirit to cleanse you anew, and then to invade your life these next seven days. Ask Him all the days long to call you back and back into a renewed awareness of Himself; but put the burden of initiation squarely on Him. Tell Him, "Lord, I'll never remember You at all unless You call me!"

Wrote Henri Nouwen:

> Every day I see again that only You can teach me to pray, only You can set my heart at rest, only You can let me dwell in Your presence.
>
> No book, no idea, no concept or theory will ever bring me close to You unless You Yourself are the One who lets these instruments become the way to You.[1]

24

Reading for Day One

This business of Christ's being "Immanuel, God with us" is full of meaning. In Old English "with" was not only a preposition but a noun. Listen to JUDGES 16:6,7 in the old King James Version:

> *Delilah said to Samson, "Tell me, I pray thee, wherein thy great strength lieth, and wherewith thou mightest be bound to afflict thee."*
>
> *And Samson said unto her, "If they bind me with seven green withs that were never dried, then shall I be weak, and be as another man."*

A "with," in former days, was what people called a young, supple vine so tough that it was used like twine to tie things together.

God is "with" you: He is bound to you; you can feel Him; He can feel you; where one of you goes, the other goes.

> . . . And round my heart still closely twined
> Those cords which naught can sever;

> For I am His and He is mine
> Forever and forever![1]

God "with" you!

Each Haven of Rest radio program ends with these words: "Go with God; He goes with you."
Sings the old tune,

> My God and I go through the fields together;
> we walk and talk as good friends should,
> and do. . . .

These next 24 hours, walk and talk together. He is *with* you.

25

Reading for Day Two

JOHN 1:1 says a deep thing:

> *The Word [Christ, before the beginning of time] was*
> *with God, and the Word was God.*

"With" in the original Greek rendering of this verse
could read "The Word was facing God," or "The Word was
face-to-face with God." It implies closest friendship, intimacy.

When Christ says to you, "Surely I am with you always" (MATTHEW 28:20), in a sense He's saying He is with
you face-to-face. His face is affectionately close to your face,
in the same one-on-one, happy, communing relationship
and fellowship that Christ the Word knew with God before
the foundation of the world.

> *Anne:* I've never had much success witnessing to hair-
> dressers because they're always above and behind
> me as they work on my hair, and they have one eye
> on what's going on around them. On the other
> hand, I've led several manicurists to Christ; we sit

face-to-face for at least half an hour at a time, giving each other our undivided attention.

That's the way God is with you, believer—not over your head, near but above you somewhere, with His mind simultaneously on many other people and situations. He is face-to-face . . . *with you*.

Oh, the blessing—think about it—that we bestow when we give each other the Aaronic benediction (NUMBERS 6:24-26):

> *The Lord bless you*
>   *and keep you;*
> *the Lord make his face shine upon you*
>   *and be gracious to you;*
> *the Lord turn his face toward you*
>   *and give you peace.*

The two of us also have the feeling that on that glorious day when we see Him literally, we won't just be part of some huge throng, maybe stuck somewhere in the back row where we can barely see Him. Somehow—somehow—we believe each child of His will be with Him "face to face" (1 CORINTHIANS 13:12). Our sin gone and mortality behind us, we'll be in our resurrection bodies which can "see him as he is" (1 JOHN 3:2)—and we won't even need telescopes!

Recognize Him face-to-face with you at this moment— and through this day.

26

Reading for Day Three

What difference will it make this day in your life if you actually "practice His presence," conscious that He is Immanuel, "God with" you?

Think of Joseph in the Old Testament. He knew the presence of God in His "up" times:

> *The Lord was with Joseph and he prospered, and he lived in the house of his Egyptian master* (GENESIS 39:2).

But Joseph also knew God's presence in his "down" times:

> *But while Joseph was there in the prison, the Lord was with him* (GENESIS 39:20, 21).

God's presence, His aroma, His flavor, His style, His constant, loving companionship was ever within and surrounding Joseph. And that shaped him, strengthened him, taught him, encouraged him, and moved him steadily forward.

No wonder Joseph could say later to his troublers,

> *You intended to harm me, but God intended it for good* (GENESIS 50:20).

And at the end, his old father Jacob summarized Joseph's life like this:

> *With bitterness archers attacked him;*
>   *they shot at him with hostility.*
> *But his bow remained steady,*
>   *his strong arms stayed limber,*
> *because of the hand of the Mighty One of Jacob*
>   (GENESIS 39:23–25).

What will the next 24 hours bring to you? Whether "up" times or "down" times or both, you're safe. And in either, be content. God is *with you.* All is well.

Wrote Brother Lawrence, "Lord, I am Yours. Dryness does not matter or affect me."[1]

27

Reading for Day Four

There's something God is trying to tell us about the connection between His presence and light. We two don't see it yet, and we suspect nobody does perfectly. But something wonderful is definitely there.

When Jesus Christ intercepted Saul on the Damascus road, "suddenly a light from heaven flashed around him" (ACTS 9:3)—a light so bright it blinded him.

When Christ had earlier been transfigured on the mountaintop before the three disciples, "his face shone like the sun, and his clothes became as white as the light" (MATTHEW 17:2)—and the original Greek indicates the light was a pulsating, flashing light.

When the apostle John got a glimpse of heaven, he saw that "from the throne came flashes of lightning" (REVELATION 4:5).

David's psalm said:

> Out of the brightness of his presence
> bolts of lightning blazed forth (2 SAMUEL 22:13).

When Ezekiel had a vision of Him he testified that he saw "an immense cloud with flashing lightning and surrounded by brilliant light" (EZEKIEL 1:4).

Daniel reported that "his face [was] like lightning" (DANIEL 10:6).

Is all this just speaking metaphorically—like "your word is a lamp to my feet and a light for my path" in PSALM 119:105? Maybe. But then how would you explain the following—

When God met Moses on Mount Sinai:

> *To the Israelites the glory of the Lord looked like a consuming fire on top of the mountain* (EXODUS 24:17).

And God's guiding them through the desert was described like this:

> *The Lord went ahead of them . . . by night in a pillar of fire to give them light* (EXODUS 13:21).

REVELATION 21:23 says of the New Jerusalem:

> *The city does not need the sun or the moon to shine on it, for the glory of God gives it light.*

REVELATION 22:5 repeats the same thing. And Ezekiel describes in his prophetic vision of the return of the Lord:

> *The land [will be] radiant with his glory* (EZEKIEL 43:2).

PSALM 104:2 says that God "wraps himself in light as with a garment." FIRST TIMOTHY 6:16 says that He "lives in unapproachable light." FIRST JOHN 1:5 says simply, "God is light."

All this may still indeed be metaphor. Just the same, have a little awe in your heart as you identify with those blessed ones of PSALM 89:15:

> *Blessed are those . . .*
> *who walk in the light of your presence, O Lord.*

If this *isn't* entirely metaphorical, there may be more to this practicing His presence than we have realized.

Now read with even deeper appreciation:

> *The Lord bless you*
> *and keep you;*
> *The Lord make his face shine upon you . . .*
> *The Lord turn his face toward you . . .* (NUMBERS 6:24–26).

Is this what made Moses' face radiant?

Will He make your face radiant today?

28

Reading for Day Five

In His presence, living this day will look different to you; sin will look different to you. In secret we can be tempted to do things we would never do if others were present.

Well, *He will be present all day.* Christ will be with you each moment, in each place, as actually as He was in the Garden or sitting at the table in the upper room.

Jeremy Taylor says, with tongue in cheek, if you're determined to sin, go where God is not:

> Be sure while you are in His sight you behave yourself as becomes so holy a presence. But if you will sin, retire yourself wisely and go where God cannot see, for nowhere else can you be safe.[1]

Suppose you're standing around in a public place with a group of people, and suddenly several black limousines stop at the curb outside your building. A "front man" hops out, comes to the door, and explains that the President of the United States is 20 minutes ahead of his planned schedule and is going to drop in.

Everyone is quickly searched, all identities are noted down, and then a group of dark-suited men casually stroll in. Among the bodyguards, there he is. You would know him anywhere; you've seen him hundreds of times on television.

For 20 minutes he shakes hands and chats. He may speak directly to you, or he may not, but in the company of the President of the United States, wouldn't you stand taller? If you itched somewhere, would you scratch? And wouldn't your conversation, even to other people, be on a higher plane? You would suddenly feel important. Life would be loftier.

Simple illustration, but you get the point.

> *Let your gentleness [or your gentlemanliness—*
> *your good breeding, your moderation, your holy*
> *living] be evident to all. The Lord is near*
> (PHILIPPIANS 4:5).

Sin will keep you from the felt presence of God, or the felt presence of God will keep you from sin. Even this very day.

29

Reading for Day Six

In God's presence this day, walk released, walk in liberty.

> *Where the Spirit of the Lord is, there is freedom*
> (2 CORINTHIANS 3:17).

> *The Spirit of the Lord is upon me [announced Christ] . . .*
> *to proclaim freedom for the prisoners* (LUKE 4:18).

The Spirit has released all Christians from slavery and fear (ROMANS 8:15) and given them a spirit of glorious freedom (ROMANS 8:21)—unless they insist on refusing their benefits.

Carnal Christians continue to live as full of fears and guilt as in their old preconversion days. That's why they're called "worldly"; they've never let themselves be sprung loose from the shackling attitudes of the world. They're hostile. They're inhibited. They're suspicious. They're threatened. They're chained to man-made rules and regulations. They're bound up in worries, self-doubts, and what-ifs.

The opposite—living deliberately in God's presence—is living again in the Garden of Eden! It returns us to the liberating, joyous lifestyle that Adam and Eve knew before their fall. But worldliness drives us out from His felt presence and from His fellowship. We're banished to "work the ground" (GENESIS 3:23) and to live in a cursed situation (GENESIS 3:17–19), full of restrictions and frustrations (GENESIS 3:24).

David Hazard prays, "Help me walk again in a paradise of peace with You."[1]

> It is for freedom that Christ has set us free [says GALATIANS 5:1]. Stand firm, then, and do not let yourselves be burdened again by a yoke of slavery!

Sons aren't slaves; sons have an altogether different self-image. They're free to rush into their father's presence at any time and be familiar with him. They know they're accepted and loved.

Slaves and hired help find their freedom only on their days off, when they're temporarily released from their duties. Sons find their freedom *in the midst of* their duties.

But don't make the mistake of thinking that your high status as a son gives you the freedom to decide whether you're going to obey Him or not, do your duties or not!

Writes Puritan John Owen:

> The liberty of sons is in the inward spiritual freedom of their hearts, gladly and willingly obeying God in everything.[2]

Your privileged position gives you *power* to obey Him this new day. And your God-given love for Him gives you *joy* in obeying Him this new day.

Go into these next 24 hours delighted to please and love God, even as God is delighted to please and love you.

30

Reading for Day Seven

This next new day in the presence of God, think about the tremendous status, title, and privileges you've been given as a son of your heavenly Father.

Do you remember Abraham's and Sarah's delight in the son God gave them? They even named him Isaac, meaning "laughter"; they were thrilled beyond words.

But what a difference with little Ishmael: Ishmael bugged Sarah to death. He was the slave-woman's child, and Sarah couldn't stand to have him around, apparently on even terms with little Isaac, the true son, and enjoying all the same rights and privileges. Eventually she actually had him driven out; she felt it was inappropriate for him to be in his father's presence.

Isaac's rights, on the other hand, were freely his. He got birthday parties described as "great feasts" (GENESIS 21:8). No lengths were spared to get him the best possible wife (GENESIS 24). His father's possessions, reputation, rights, privileges, power, and status were all his. He was the much-loved son, happy, obedient, and fully at ease in the pleasure of his father's presence.

The prodigal son of Luke 15 lived under exactly the same terms, but unlike Isaac he actually volunteered to get out! It was the mistake of his life, and he ended up in a pig-pen. Although he was a fully legitimate son, it was only when he got back to his father's presence again, humbled, repentant, and broken, that the "good life" resumed: good clothes, jewelry, fine food, and parties with music and dancing. God isn't exaggerating when He says that "in his presence is fullness of joy; at his right hand are pleasures forevermore" (PSALM 16:11 KJV).

Oh, friend, this next 24 hour period,

> *Enter his gates with thanksgiving*
> *and his courts with praise;*
> *give thanks to him and praise his name.*
> *For the Lord is good and his love endures forever*
> (PSALM 100:4,5).

Move in close—humble, appreciative, and thankful.

Live with joy in His love.

And then keep doing this for eternity. That's your new assignment.

Would you let us know how you're doing? We'd like to hear from you.

Warmly in Christ,

Ray and Anne Ortlund
4500 Campus Drive, Suite 662
Newport Beach, California 92660
U.S.A.

Epilogue

"Life from the Center is a life of unhurried peace and power. It is simple. It is serene. It is amazing. It is triumphant. It is radiant. It takes no time, but it occupies all our time. And it makes our life programs new and overcoming. We need not get frantic. He is at the helm. And when our little day is done we lie down quietly in peace, for all is well."[1]

> The light of God surrounds me;
> The love of God enfolds me;
> The power of God protects me;
> The presence of God watches over me;
> Wherever I am, God is.[2]

I am to the point that a peace of soul and rest of spirit descend upon me even when I am asleep. To be without this sense, this constant sense of peace, would be suffering indeed; but with peace in my inner being I believe I could find consolation [anywhere].

No, I do not know what God purposes with me, nor what is in store for me. But I am in a calm so great that I fear nothing. What could I fear? I am with Him . . . in His presence.[3]

—Brother Lawrence (Nicholas Herman)
of France, 1611–1691

Study Guide
For Personal Reflection or
Group Discussions

It is essential not only to read God's truth but to do it
(James 1:22)—and that's why we have included these questions, to get the message and the flavor of this book "deep
into your bones." We encourage you either to answer these
questions on your own as you read through the book or else
to use them in a small group study. In either case you'll be
helped if you jot down what you're learning in a notebook
for later filing and reuse.

> *The precepts of the Lord are right....*
> *By them is your servant warned;*
>   *in keeping them there is great reward....*
> *May the words of my mouth and the meditation of*
>   *my heart*
> *be pleasing in your sight,*
> *O LORD, my Rock and my Redeemer.*
>   —PSALM 19;8,11,14

Questions for Session 1 (Chapter 1)

- In reading Brother Lawrence's book, Ray and Anne made some decisions: "Attention to God was to be not just a slot of time every day, but all day long, every day. His presence was to permeate everything. We would commit ourselves to do everything for the love of God, in simple rest and without fear" (p. 3).

  —How would living out such a vow change your own day-to-day life? Your attitude toward tough times and difficult people? Your perspective on life's challenges? Your approach to those exhausting, frustrating, boring, seemingly hopeless or pointless moments of life you sometimes encounter?

  —What does "Living in His presence is the secret to living" mean to you?

- Frank Laubach, Bernard of Clairvaux, David Hazard, W.Y. Fullerton, Francis of Assisi, and Thomas Kelly, as well as Adam and Eve before the fall, Abraham, Isaac, Jacob, Moses, Joshua, David, Ezekiel, Daniel, and the apostle John—these people also experienced the presence of God (pp. 6–8).

  —Which quote speaks most powerfully to you? Why?

  —Whom have you met—in your reading or in real life—who clearly knows God's presence? What evidence led you to that conclusion? What impact has this person had on you and your spiritual life?

—Missionary Frank Laubach wrote in his diary, "I could find nobody who could wholly understand me except God." When have you found that to be true?

—Think about all that's going on in your life today. What do you have a hard time explaining? What do people have a hard time understanding? In regard to what situation do you find it especially comforting that God understands you? Why would this truth about God's ability to know and understand you draw you closer to him?

—What goals and hopes for your spiritual life prompted you to begin reading this book?

Questions for Session 2 (Chapter 2)

• God wants you to be made perfect in love, and the foundation of this promise is His love for you, not your love for him. God's love for you is purer, stronger, larger, and more persistent than you can even imagine (p. 10).

—Describe your understanding of God's love for you personally. Is your concept based on the truth of the Bible or has it been skewed by life's hard times, your relationship with your father, or something else?

—Read through the following truths from Scripture. What do they teach about God's love?

> PSALM 100:5; 103:8; 107:8
> JOHN 15:13
> ROMANS 5:8
> 1 CORINTHIANS 13:1–13
> 1 JOHN 3:1

—You have just looked at the truth about God's love. Why would such knowledge of God's love help motivate you to practice His presence?

—Whether you're aware of it or not, God's love surrounds you (PSALM 32:10) and supports you (PSALM 94:18). As the psalmist proclaims, "The earth is filled with his love" (119:64). What will you do to become more aware of the evidence of God's love?

• As you continue to look at the truth about God's love, look more closely at JOHN 3:16 and, as suggested in the text, think about the emotions behind the words (pp. 12, 13).

—*"God so loved the world. . . . "* When has your love for someone motivated you to act sacrificially and selflessly? Give one or two examples. Reflect on your feelings at the time.

—"... *that he gave his one and only Son* ..." What have you loved deeply but nevertheless sacrificed for someone? Give an example. Now imagine someone you love deeply. What feelings come when you think about sending him or her to a sacrificial death?

—"... *that whoever believes in him* ..." Do you believe in Jesus? Have you named Him your Lord and Savior? If not, do so now by simply admitting to Him your need for Him, asking Him to forgive your sin, and inviting Him to be Lord of your life. If you have already named Jesus as Lord, explain how John 3:16 is not only an invitation to salvation, but also an urging to sanctification. How does believing in Jesus facilitate you becoming more like Him?

—"... *shall not perish but have eternal life.*" What images, emotions, and thoughts come when you hear the phrase "eternal life"? What relationship do you imagine having with Jesus forever? Know that this relationship starts now!

Questions for Session 3 (Chapters 3, 4)

- God's love for you is far richer than any human love because, when He loves you to the utmost (JOHN 13:1), He is loving you infinitely. Acting on this love, God has washed you perfectly clean from your sin and made you perfectly acceptable to Him (p. 16).

—ZEPHANIAH 3:17 reads, "He will quiet you with his love." Read John Owen's explanation of this verse (pages 16, 17). Look also at Hebrews 10:15–18. What unconfessed sins can you lay before God today? Now thank Him for His forgiveness and for a silence which means that, as He looks at you in Jesus Christ, He no longer has any complaints against you.

—When God forgives and erases your sin, He also clothes you in God's righteousness through Christ (ROMANS 4:5). What kind of relationship with God does this righteousness allow to happen? What kind of role in the world does this righteousness call for?

• Our God is infinite in His goodness, His love, His wisdom, His power, His knowledge, His grace—His very being. God loves you, forgives you, saves you, cleanses you, and superintends your life with the capacity of God. To help your finite mind grasp these immeasurable truths, consider these five statements from Chapter 2:

God delights in you and . . . He loves to have you in His presence.

The Lord "rejoices in his works" (PSALM 104:31), including you.

He who knows you best loves you most.

He wants you to live in His joyous presence not only later, but now.

We continually sin, but He continually cleanses (pp. 16–21).

—Which of these statements speaks most loudly to you today? Why? What half-truth about God's love for you are you wrestling with right now?

—What does it mean to you that God loves you, forgives you, saves you, cleanses you, and superintends your life with the capacity of God? Why, for instance, is it significant that *God Himself* is doing these things for you rather than a mere human being?

• We sinful human beings are not fit to enter into the presence of our Creator, the Most High and Holy God. The prophet Isaiah knew that, but he went on to explain so much more (pp. 22–24).

—Read ISAIAH 6:1–5. How does Isaiah react to his vision of the Lord seated upon His heavenly throne? When have you been most aware of God's holiness and therefore of your own sinfulness? Describe the situation as well as your reaction to God's purity and goodness and also to your uncleanness.

—In the Old Testament, this stark contrast between God's holiness and human sinfulness meant that only the high priest could enter the room of God's presence, the Holy of Holies, and he could do so only once a year (HEBREWS 9:3–7). When have you not been allowed to enter a place? What reasons were given? What did you feel when the door remained closed to you?

—Now read ISAIAH 63:1–5. What does Isaiah see when he looks at Jesus? What does Jesus say about the reason His garments are red?

—Now what does the fact that Jesus' garments were red—the fact that He died on the cross—mean for you personally? Remember the Holy of Holies which you have been forbidden to enter.

—What meaning do Jesus' words in JOHN 14:6— "I am the way and the truth and the life. No one comes to the Father except by me"—take on against the background of ISAIAH 63?

• Look again at the words of Frank Laubach as he reports people's reactions to his goal of "trying to line up my actions with the will of God about every fifteen minutes or every half hour" (p. 22).

—What was your initial reaction to the missionary's goal?

—What is your thinking about the goal now that you have considered the Way to God's presence? Remember, too, the promise of JAMES 4:8.

Questions for Session 4 (Chapters 5, 6)

- Why all the doctrine in the beginning of a book on practicing the presence of God? Because doctrine must come before application. Application which doesn't flow out of doctrine is like a cut flower: It is without continuing nourishment and it is dying (pp. 27, 28).

  —What do you think of when you hear the word "doctrine"? What is your attitude toward its value? What have you learned from or been reminded of in this discussion of the importance of doctrine?

  —Take a pop quiz. Summarize your understanding of some of the great truths of the gospel: justification by faith; sanctification; imputed righteousness; heaven and hell; prophecy; Jesus as the incarnate God; the Trinity. What do your hesitant answers—if any—tell you about what you need to study and review?

- We who have recognized Jesus as the source of our forgiveness and the Way to God's presence are now to "grow in the grace and knowledge of our Lord and Savior Jesus Christ" (2 PETER 3:18; see pp. 27–29).

  —Explain the statement "What you believe about God—your theology—is what shapes and defines the real you."

—Remember Roy Castle on his deathbed? When have you seen illustrated in real life the truth that our beliefs shape our behaviors and words?

—What are you doing to continue to "grow in the grace and knowledge" of Jesus? Or what will you start doing today?

- A full day of work and rushing around; a relaxing evening of dinner out and a movie; battles with sleeplessness, taking off weight, and shingles— whatever the circumstances of our life, our position "in Christ" never changes (p. 30).

—In what easy, wonderful moments of grace have you been aware that you were "in Christ"?

—Sometimes we are more aware of being "in Christ" during life's more difficult times. When has that been true for you? When has it been anything but true for you? When has God seemed quite absent during life's trials?

—What do the preceding two questions remind you about the fickleness of feelings and the importance of knowing the doctrinal truth that you are in Jesus and He is in you (JOHN 14:20)?

- In JOHN 15, Jesus tells us to abide in him (verses 4,5,9,10). Abiding in Him isn't automatic behavior or He wouldn't command it (p. 31)!

—What particular events or circumstances tend to make you forget that you are abiding in Christ and instead get you living like an orphan—fussing, worrying, and struggling in your own strength?

—How are you doing today? Are you abiding in Christ? Or are you fussing, worrying, and struggling in your own strength? Pray for each other—for yourself—about this.

Questions for Session 5 (Chapters 7, 8)

- Do you find the fact that God is invisible an obstacle to His presence? Consider the fact that the immortal part of you—the conscious part of you that is free to interact with God—is also invisible (pp. 35, 36)!

  —What does the Bible teach about the relationship between your body and the real you? (See, for instance, 1 CORINTHIANS 6:19; 15:42–44.)

  —Describe the *real* you.

- God is always here and He is always simultaneously elsewhere. In a word, God is omnipresent, filling heaven and earth, being right by your side at the same time that He is with those you love (JEREMIAH 23:23,24; see p. 36).

  —Are you like the baby in the high chair when it comes to receiving God's nourishing presence? Are your lips a

hard, tight line, impossible to penetrate? If so, why—
and what will you do to relax your resistance?

- The pressures and pace of life can seem to form an
obstacle to practicing the presence of God, but
think for a moment of who is with you as you go
about your fast-paced, full life (p. 38).

  —As you think about God, read PSALM 90:4. Describe the pace at which He, the eternal One, does
  things and His perspective on time.

  —In case you didn't stop as you read the text—
  and, being a busy person, you probably didn't—
  stop now and say together as a group or on your
  own, *"God* loves me." Talk or think about that
  amazing truth. Then say "God *loves* me" and consider the implications of that fact. Finally, say "God
  loves *me"* and marvel at the wondrous grace.

  —It's not work or a busy pace that debilitates—it's
  only a wrong attitude toward that work and that
  pace. One wrong attitude that many busy twentieth-century Christians fall into is not honoring the
  Lord's Sabbath-rest (HEBREWS 4:9–11). What do
  you do to keep this rest? What do you think God
  might want you to be doing?

  —What do you do to find rest in the Lord on any
  day of the week? What do you think God might
  want you to be doing?

- Practicing the presence of God isn't something to add to your already busy schedule. It doesn't take *more* of your time—it takes *all* of your time. It's what you do while you're doing what you're doing (p. 40).

—Jacob was engrossed in life's journey—its pain, its challenges, its worries—when suddenly he realized the reality of the Lord's presence with him (GENESIS 28:16). When have you suddenly been reminded of God's presence with you? How did you respond? How did that realization change your life, even if only temporarily?

—Why does it make sense that, as you dwell in the presence of God, your life will gradually rearrange itself? Why does this promise encourage and/or unsettle you? What will you do to test the statement's truth?

Questions for Session 6 (Chapters 9, 10)

- Looking at who God is—in all His power, glory, and splendor—can be all we need to cure us of our pride (pp. 42–46).

—What in your life tends to be a source of unhealthy pride, a pride which nurtures a feeling of self-sufficiency and discourages reliance on God and abiding in His presence?

—Review the following six truths about God:

All power is of God (2 CHRONICLES 20:6).
All money and possessions are of God (PSALM 50:12; COLOSSIANS 1:16).
All wisdom is of God (ROMANS 11:33–36).
All energy is of God (HEBREWS 1:3; JOB 34:14,15).
All life and all health are of God (JOHN 1:4, 5:26).
All forgiveness is of God (MARK 2:7; PSALM 130:4).

In which statements do you find an antidote to the pride you just confessed?

—Which of these six statements especially invite you to practice God's presence? Why do you think those speak to your heart?

• Practicing the presence of God is a humble, modest, and (as Dietrich Bonhoeffer noted) hidden thing. It is also something we are able to do only by the gracious work of the Holy Spirit (pp. 45–47).

—Explain your understanding of Brother Lawrence's statement that we are not to try to advance faster than grace.

—Read PHILIPPIANS 2:12,13. What is your role ("continue to work out your salvation") even as

"God . . . works in you to will and to act according to his good purpose"? Describe the partnership, addressing specifically the practice of God's presence.

- God is with us and always will be (MATTHEW 1:23; 28:20), and He gives us "everything we need for life and godliness" (2 PETER 1:3). Nevertheless, we often fail to yield our will to Him and instead insist on going our own way (p. 48).

  —In what aspect of your life are you currently going your own way rather than yielding yourself to God's guidance and instruction? Pray for each other, or alone, about this.

  —Now review the scenes in LUKE 15:5,6,17–25; EXODUS 24:9–11; 1 CHRONICLES 29:20–22; JOHN 21:1-12; and REVELATION 3:20. How does God respond when His people—when you, His child—humbly enter His presence and confess their sin?

  —According to the parable of the wedding banquet in MATTHEW 22:1–14 (specifically verse 13), what happens when we don't enter humbly and penitently, on God's terms?

- Repentance is more than just lip service. Genuine repentance is a 180-degree change of direction (pp. 50–52).

—What inner struggle are you experiencing as you consider making that change? Where will you turn for the help and support you need to end your rebellion—or resolve your boredom, staleness, carnality, or distance—and so emerge victorious in that battle?

Questions for Session 7 (Chapter 11)

- Getting to anything worthwhile means getting past the distractions, and four obvious distractions can greatly interfere with our practice of the presence of God (pp. 53–59).

  —Our sin, our bad theology, sudden bad news, and the idea that practicing the presence of God will be too exhausting—these can indeed distract us from our efforts to abide in the Lord. Which distractions (these and any others) do you face?

  —*Sin:* What can you learn from Jesus about how to stand strong against Satan's temptations (LUKE 4:1–13)? What can you learn from Brother Lawrence about how to deal with your sin so that it doesn't come between you and God (pages 53, 54 of the text)?

  —*Bad Theology:* What is your understanding of how much God is interested in the details—the problems, the pressures, the sources of fear—in your life? How does this theology, right or wrong, affect your attitude toward practicing His presence? What will you do to straighten out bad theology?

—*Bad News:* What unexpected calamity, if any, has prompted you to shift into your independence mode in an effort to survive? What does PSALM 46:1 remind you?

—*The Idea That Practicing the Presence of God Will Be Exhausting:* Are you sensing that practicing the presence of God will be a lot of work? First, what does the analogy of the bird's wings say to you (page 58)? What does Oswald Sanders' statement, "The world is run by tired people," mean to you? And why does it make sense that God's people— even when they're tired—can accomplish a lot for His kingdom?

- Our perception of God's unreality, the pressures and pace of life, our pride, our unyielding and unyielded wills, and the distractions that come our way—these things can indeed be obstacles to practicing God's presence (pp. 53–59).

—What does EPHESIANS 6:10–18 teach about how to stand strong against obstacles like these?

—Take time now to pray for each other, or alone, for strength in these battles.

Questions for Session 8 (Chapters 12, 13)

- Our Almighty God can communicate to people any way He wishes. For some that might mean hearing voices and seeing visions. But such ecstatic experiences aren't necessary for practicing God's presence (pp. 63, 64).

  —First, God has revealed His truth in His Holy Scriptures. When has God clearly communicated to you through His Word? Give one or two examples.

  —Second, God has given us the Holy Spirit to teach us as we study the Bible. When has the Holy Spirit taught you something through the written or preached Word? Again, give a specific example or two.

  —Have these sources of knowledge about God— His Word and His Spirit—been sufficient for you? When have the words of Scripture and/or the indwelling of the Holy Spirit made you confident of God's presence and thereby strengthened you in the "down" times when you "feel" nothing at all of God's presence?

- You can always trust sound doctrine and the truth that God is with you now and forever. You can't always trust experience and feelings (pp. 64–67).

—When have you cried out as Anne did, "O God! Have you let us to wander on our own?" When have you, like David, asked, "Why, O Lord, do you stand far off? Why do you hide yourself in times of trouble?" (PSALM 10:1)?

—What role did the Bible play in helping you again assert confidently that "you hear, O Lord, the desire of the afflicted; you encourage them, and you listen to their cry" (PSALM 10:17)? What role did the Holy Spirit play? How did God use His people in your life during those dark days? What comfort did you find in doctrine (head knowledge about God) even as your heart was breaking?

• Turning your face toward God is hardly turning your back on reality—on sin, suffering, and death. After all, our loving and gracious God grieves over these sins, but He also waits to act on His righteous wrath, judging and punishing evildoers, and is always at work to redeem these losses (pp. 68–71).

—What do DEUTERONOMY 32:39, ISAIAH 45:7, and 1 SAMUEL 2:6,7 teach about our Sovereign God, our merciful but righteously angry God, our compassionate but just God?

—Bob Pierce, founder of World Vision, once said, "Let my heart be broken with the things that break the heart of God." How can practicing the presence of God be a step toward having this prayer answered? And what does this prayer suggest about whether or not drawing near to God is a means of escape from the harsh realities of our sin-filled world?

- The simplicity which God wants His children to experience is not childlike naiveté or blissful ignorance. It is the simplicity of maturity in God. It is the simplicity of letting God be God, of looking to Jesus knowing that spiritual warfare rages and that He will ultimately triumph (pp. 72–74).

—When has God sheltered you from the harsh winds of life and been a refuge when its storms have raged around you (ISAIAH 32:2)? Was your turning to Him escapism? Obedience? An act of desperation? An act of spiritual maturity? Explain—and share what you learned about God from the experience.

—What current situations—in the world at large and in your life in particular—do you need to see from the Bible's vantage point that a good and redemptive God is at work? Make the items on your list the topic of a prayer right now.

Questions for Session 9 (Chapter 14)

- Long ago God purposed in His heart to come down and live with His creation, the men and women He fashioned with His hands. Through the death and resurrection of His Son, the Lord Jesus Christ, God forged an even greater intimacy: He actually dwells within His people (pp. 75–80).

  —If you are a Christian, God the Father dwells in you (1 JOHN 4:15). If you are a Christian, Jesus Christ dwells in you (COLOSSIANS 1:27). And if you are a Christian, the Holy Spirit dwells in you (2 CORINTHIANS 1:21,22). What does each of these three truths mean for you and how you can live your life?

  —When has God's power at work in your life been especially obvious to you (EPHESIANS 3:20,21)? When has your knowledge of God's love been especially comforting and encouraging (EPHESIANS 3:17–19)? When have you seen evidence of the Spirit's fruit in your life (GALATIANS 5:22,23)? Praise your indwelling God for His presence in you!

- Trying to determine whether or not to leave Lake Avenue Congregational Church after 20 years there was a significant crossroads, but once Anne and Ray were in agreement, God was speaking through everyone to tell them to move on (pp. 80–83).

—When have you heard God say, "Move" and obeyed even though you had no idea where you were going? What did you learn about God from that faith-building experience?

—Where is God calling you to move today? Where is He calling you to take a step of faith? What does the fact that Jesus is Immanuel, "God with you," mean in this situation? How does the truth of God's constant presence with you encourage and even enable you to give yourself completely to Him who, after all, gave Himself completely to you?

Questions for Session 10 (Chapters 15–17)

• The practice of God's presence means deciding to believe that He is with you whether or not you sense it. It's a commitment you make as you acknowledge that He is with you now and from every moment on (p. 88).

—When have you had a Saipan experience, a time when you knew that God's presence was very real? Be specific about the event, God's work, and your reaction.

—Have you decided to believe that God is with you whether or not you sense it as powerfully as you did in the scene you just described? If so, has believing become seeing? Explain any new sensitivity to God's presence in your life.

- To feel God's presence, to meet Him in special times and intimate ways, to experience the overshadowing of His Holy Spirit in power—this has been the desire of God's people since the beginning. And it is this longing that David and the other writers of the Psalms are talking about when they speak of wanting to be in God's house, His tent, His courts, and His temple (pp. 88–90).

  —Review some of the psalms and their references to places where God resides (27:4; 61:4; 23:6; 63:2; 15:1,2; 84:2,4,10). When you replace the noun ("house," "tent," "courts," "temple") with the idea of God's presence, which words of prayer and praise could be your own expression of desire?

  —Perhaps this twentieth-century restatement of the sentiment of PSALM 84 sounds more like you: "Lord, I'm at church all the time, but I'm not satisfied to be merely serving inside four walls. I long for Your very presence." State this desire in your own words.

- Ralph Cushman quotes Phillips Brooks as saying, "It is no figure of speech. . . . He is here. I know Him. He knows me. It is the realest thing in the world, and every day it grows realer" (p. 93).

—When has God's presence with you, your knowledge of God, and/or His knowledge of you been most real? Reflect on what you may have done to be able to receive that moment of grace.

—The knowledge of God's presence will cheer you, but the *practice* of His presence will revolutionize you. Why would being in touch with God's presence revolutionize you? What impact might that awareness of His realness have on you? Imagine the effect, and remember that God is "able to do immeasurably more than all we ask or imagine" (EPHESIANS 3:20)!

—Why does the practice of God's presence enliven one's consciousness of personal sin and renew one's longing to be holy?

—Why does the practice of God's presence bring comfort and happiness as well as a heightened "fear of the Lord"?

• In PSALM 16:8–11, David shares his own experience of the presence of God, an experience which may further encourage you to practice being aware of His closeness to you each moment of the day (pp. 94, 95).

—David says, "I have set the Lord always before me" (verse 8). Why would each of the following be a logical, natural consequence of doing so?

"I will not be shaken" (verse 8)

"My heart is glad" (verse 9)

"My tongue rejoices" (verse 9)

"My body also will rest secure" (verse 9)

—Through PROVERBS 3:6, God calls us to acknowledge Him "in all [our] ways." What will you do to practice God's presence as you work at your desk, clean the house, drive the car, cook, garden, care for the children, etc.? How will you acknowledge Him as you go about the various activities of your day?

• Besides giving us a few quiet moments with God, writing out our daily prayers can also serve as a reminder of where we've been, how God has met us and helped us, and what God has done in our lives (pp. 97, 98).

—What words and phrases in this chapter's prayers touch your heart? Which words and phrases could be your own?

—Who in your life witnesses to you of God and His goodness? After this meeting or meditation, let them know, too, just how much you appreciate them!

—What encouragement for the practice of the presence of God do you find in these prayers? Consider, for instance, the Scripture references and the very personal testimony. Should you consider writing your own daily prayers?

Questions for Session 11 (Chapters 18, 19)

- When he first heard about practicing the presence of God, the manager of a local hamburger place decided he and God were going to cook hamburgers together. When he became sharply aware of God's presence, missionary David Brainard rededicated himself to the Lord. And when Job suffered terrible losses, he found himself at a point where he saw the Lord (Job 42:5; see pp. 99–102).

  —Is yours a secondhand faith, or have you come to know and enjoy a personal relationship with Almighty God? Talk about why you may be stuck with merely a secondhand faith or about what people, events, and experiences with the Lord have helped move you along to a genuine personal relationship with God.

  —What goals do you have for your spiritual growth? How can practicing the presence of God help you reach those goals?

- Oswald Chambers has observed the following: "First God gives us a vision; then He takes us down into the valley and batters us into the shape of the vision. And it is in the valley that so many of us faint and give way" (p. 102).

  —Which men and women of the Bible come to mind as you read the beginning of Mr. Chambers'

statement? Who has God taken into the valley?
What battering did that person experience? And
how did that experience make him or her more the
person God designed him to be?

—Which of the tough times in your life does this
statement above put into perspective? What was
God doing in your soul and your character during
those dark days in the valley? How did you hold
up? Did you "faint and give way"? Why or why not?
What role did your awareness of God's presence
play in whether or not you fainted and gave way?

- The fellowship of God's presence is a sweet theo-
cratic union, where Christ rules, directs, and guides
the network of people who have been invaded by
God and are therefore God-enthralled (p. 104).

  —According to Jesus' words in JOHN 14:23,24,
  what is the one criterion that needs to be met if a
  person is to enjoy the fellowship of God's presence
  and His people?

  —Remember the story of Gideon's army? God in-
  structed Gideon to pare down the original 32,000
  men to 300—and then gave the soldiers a great victory over the Midianites. Why did God reduce the
  army so significantly (see JUDGES 7:2)? What lesson
  is there in this story for us, God's army of believers
  today, some of whom who might be tempted to
  boast about their close fellowship with the Lord?

- God also pared down the priesthood, eliminating the Levites who had served the Israelite people to the point of assisting them in idol worship! God wants His people to serve Him, the Lord, not their fellow people (pp. 106, 107).

  —Think about your church involvement. Where are you serving the Lord? Where are you serving people and doing the busywork of Christendom? How do these two kinds of service differ from each other? Which, for instance, is more satisfying to you? To the Lord?—Take a quick inventory of your church activities. Could some of them be "meaningless offerings" to the Lord (ISAIAH 1:13)? Which do you delight in? Which do you think the Lord delights in? Which activities will you prayerfully consider eliminating so that you can focus your energy on serving God, not people?

Questions for Session 12 (Chapters 20, 21)

- Review the account of Ray's brush with possible cancer (pp. 110–113).

  —What was the reason for the peace Ray and Anne experienced during that week of waiting for the follow-up doctor visit?

  —When have you had such an experience of being sheltered by God's presence (PSALM 31:20)?

—What role do you think the Nebraska farmer's fervent prayers that week made?

—When have you been nudged to pray for someone and then found out how critical your prayers were in his or her life?

—Summarize what Ray's "cancer" illustrates about the benefit of God's presence in believers' lives.

• When Jesus left this earth in His resurrection body, His last words were "Surely I am with you always, to the very end of the age" (MATTHEW 28:20; see p. 113).

—For what situation in the coming week is this promise of Jesus' perpetual presence with you especially encouraging? What will you do to remind yourself of God's presence with you when you deal with that situation?

—Whom do you know who—today—needs to be reminded of God's presence with him or her in the darkness? Remind him, but not with clichéd biblical truths. Does that person need a meal? A hug? A chance to get out of the house? A phone call? Some flowers? A few minutes to pray with you? Pray for each other to be guided or ask the Lord to guide you personally as you reach out.

• In case you haven't already realized it, there are no clear-cut steps, no surefire techniques, and no specific

formula for practicing God's presence. We don't
need to train ourselves to be in His presence. Instead, we are simply to acknowledge His presence
with us and start living in light of that truth (p. 115).

—What role will God's Spirit play in helping us
practice God's presence? See ROMANS 8:16 and
EPHESIANS 1:18.

—What role does faith play in the practice of God's
presence? See EPHESIANS 3:17. Contrast the role of
faith with the role of feelings in practicing God's
presence.

• The importance of faith points back to our earlier
discussion of the importance of doctrine (pp. 27,
28). Learning doctrine—investigating God's Word
until the truth of it overwhelms you and excites
you—can help you practice God's presence (p. 117).

—What are you doing to get to know God better
through His Word? What are you doing in your personal times of study? What role does worship play in
your getting to know God's Word and God Himself
better?

—What do your answers to the preceding series of
questions tell you about what you might be doing
to strengthen your walk with the Lord? What is the
first step you'll take, and when will you take it?

Questions for Session 13 (Chapter 22)

- God has always been in your life. Since before the foundation of the world, God was loving you and making plans for you (Psalm 139:15,16). Now that you have realized this truth that He is with you, you can enjoy His presence more. And you can do that by turning to Him in continual prayer and worship while you do whatever else you're doing. You also can enjoy God's presence more by constantly surrendering to Him as you detect Him making His will known throughout the day (pp. 118, 119).

  —Are you choosing to live in the presence of your problems, your needs, your irritations, and your frustrations rather than in the constant reality of God's presence with you? What role can prayer play in moving you from the first camp to the second?

  —Why should the tasks of the day, whatever they are, be able to prompt you to worship God? To pray? To seek His will and surrender to it?

- Practicing the presence of God—walking and talking with Him, aware moment by moment of His immediacy—should actually be the normal way of living for believers (pp. 119–123).

  —Why will such an awareness of God change your focus from the marginal concerns of life to the deepest issues? Why will practicing the presence of God sensitize you to what the Lord and not the world says? How will you benefit from these transformations?

—God flashed many a lightning bolt across the skies before Ben Franklin grabbed a kite and a key and figured out electricity. Likewise, God has offered evidence of His immediate presence with you even before you named His Son your Lord and Savior. Are you now moving beyond the theoretical and figuring out that you can learn to recognize Him in a new way and enjoy a new relationship with Him? What factors has God choreographed in your life to make this the moment? How will you respond?

———————————

Following Session 13 or your individual reflections, experience personally the One-Week Experiment each day this next week.

Afterward, on your own, write in your notebook your assessment of the week, when you fell short and why, and how you can move forward to more firmly establish the habit of awareness of His presence for you future. Or as a group, perhaps have a concluding dinner together for accountability and commitment.

God bless you!

Notes

Chapter 1. The Response of the Two of Us, and Many Others

1. For this story see Raymond C. Ortlund, *Lord, Make My Life a Miracle* (Ventura, CA: Regal Press, 1974).

2. Brother Lawrence and Frank Laubach, *Practicing His Presence* (The Seedsowers, P.O. Box 3568, Beaumont, TX 77704-3568), pp. 18, 19.

3. Public domain.

4. David Hazard, *A Day in Your Presence: A Forty-day Journey in the Company of Francis of Assisi* (Minneapolis: Bethany House, 1992), p. 13.

5. *The Practice of Christ's Presence* (London: Morgan and Scott Ltd., 1916), p. 4.

6. David Hazard, *A Day in Your Presence: A Forty-day Journey in the Company of Francis of Assisi* (Minneapolis: Bethany House, 1992), p. 120.

7. Thomas Kelly, *A Testament of Devotion* (New York: Harper Brothers, 1941), p. 29.

Chapter 2. The Love of God

1. Thomas Kelly, *A Testament of Devotion* (New York: Harper Brothers, 1941), p. 53.

Chapter 3. The Capacity of God

1. John Owen, *Communion with God,* abridged and made easy to read by B.J.K. Law (Edinborough, Scotland, and Carlisle, PA: the Banner of Truth Trust, 1991), p. 18.

2. Hymn, "The Solid Rock," words by Edward Mote.

3. Unknown.

4. Anne Ortlund (Dallas: Word Books, 1987).

5. Hymn, "The Love of God," words by Frederick M. Lehman, ©Copyright 1917. Renewed 1945. Nazarene Publishing House.

Chapter 4. The Way to His Presence

1. *Practicing His Presence* (The Seedsowers, P.O. Box 3568, Beaumont, TX 77704-3568), p. 2.

Chapter 7. Our Perception of God's Unreality

1. Ralph Cushman, *Practicing the Presence* (New York: Abbergdon Press, 1936), p. 48.

2. Alfred Tennyson, quoted by Ralph Cushman, ibid., p. 85.

3. Quoted from his book *Evangelism: Its Theology and Practice* in *Christianity Today,* Nov. 8, 1993.

Chapter 8. Our Pressures and Pace

1. Thomas Kelly, *A Testament of Devotion* (New York: Harper Brothers, 1941), p. 113.

Chapter 9. Our Pride

1. From Charles Wesley's hymn "Love Divine, All Loves Excelling."

Chapter 11. Our Distractions

1. Brother Lawrence and Frank Laubach, *Practicing His Presence* (The Seedsowers, P.O. Box 3568, Beaumont, TX 77704-3568), p. 46.

2. Ibid., p. 49.

3. *A Heart for God* (Colorado Springs: NavPress, 1985), p. 84.

Chapter 12. Is This Some Out-of-Body Experience?

1. Hymn, "How Firm a Foundation," words by George Keith.

2. *Practicing the Presence* (New York: Abbergdon Press, 1936), p. 83.

Chapter 13. Is the Practice of God's Presence Escapism?

1. "Spirit Quest," in *Christianity Today,* Nov. 8, 1993.

Chapter 14. How Important Is This Truth—to God and You?

1. Hymn, "How Firm a Foundation," words by George Keith.

2 *Liturgy of St. James,* fifth century; adapted by Gerand Moultrie, 1864. Public domain.

3. Hildebert of Lavardin; very old. Quoted by A.W. Tozer in The Knowledge of the Holy (New York: Harper and Row, 1961), p. 81.

Chapter 16. Elliot, Cushman, Us

1. Excerpts from Jim Elliot's Diary, *HIS,* April 1956, p. 9.

2. Ralph Cushman, *Practicing the Presence* (New York: Abbergdon Press, 1936), pp. 167–168.

3. Ibid., p. 151.

Chapter 18. The Experience of His Presence

1. ©Copyrights 1971, 1973 by Singspiration, division of The Zondervan Corporation. All rights reserved.

2. Jonathan Edwards, ed., *The Life and Diary of David Brainard,* 1744 (newly edited by Philip E. Howard, Jr., Moody Press Wycliffe Series of Christian Classics, 1949), p. 169.

3. Source unknown.

•

Chapter 22. Starting Out

1. Ralph Cushman, *Practicing the Presence* (New York: Abbergdon Press, 1936), p. 133.

2. Raymond C. Ortlund, *Lord, Make My Life a Miracle* (Ventura, CA: Regal Press, 1974).

Chapter 23. Introduction to the Week

1. Quotation from Nouwen's *A Cry for Mercy,* in Reuben P. Job and Norman Shawchuck, *A Guide to Prayer* (Nashville: The Upper Room, 1983).

Chapter 24. Reading for Day One

1. Hymn, "I've Found a Friend," public domain.

Chapter 26. Reading for Day Three

1. Brother Lawrence and Frank Laubach, *Practicing His Presence* (The Seedsowers, P.O. Box 3568, Beaumont, TX 77704-3568), p. 39.

Chapter 29. Reading for Day Six

1. *A Day in Your Presence: A Forty-day Journey in the Company of Francis of Assisi* (Minneapolis: Bethany House, 1992), p.79.

2. *Communion with God,* abridged and made easy to read by R.J.K. Law (Edinborough, Scotland, and Carlisle, PA: the Banner of Truth Trust, 1991), p. 160.

Epilogue

1. Thomas Kelly, *A Testament of Devotion* (New York: Harper Brothers, 1941), p.124.

2. Unknown.

3. Taken from Brother Lawrence and Frank Laubach, *Practicing His Presence* (The Seedsowers, P.O. Box 3568, Beaumont, TX 77704-3568), pp. 97–98.

Bibliography

Barnhouse, Donald Grey, *God's Heirs* (Grand Rapids: Eerdmans, 1963).

Brother Lawrence and Frank Laubach, *Practicing His Presence* (The Seedsowers, P.O. Box 3568, Beaumont, TX 77704-3568.

Cushman, Ralph, *Practicing the Presence* (New York: Abbergdon Press, 1936).

Edwards, Jonathan, ed., *The Life and Diary of David Brainard*, 1744 (newly edited by Philip E. Howard, Jr., Moody Press Wycliffe Series of Christian Classics, 1949).

Edwards, Jonathan, *Religious Affections* (Edinborough, Scotland, and Carlisle, PA: the Banner of Truth Trust, 1994).

Ferguson, Sinclair, *A Heart for God* (Colorado Springs: NavPress, 1985).

Fullerton, W.Y., *The Practice of Christ's Presence* (London: Morgan and Scott Ltd., 1916).

Hazard, David, *A Day in Your Presence: A Forty-day Journey in the Company of Francis of Assisi* (Minneapolis: Bethany House, 1992).

HIS, April 1956, p. 9, "Excerpts from Jim Elliot's Diary."

Kelly, Thomas, *A Testament of Devotion* (New York: Harper Brothers, 1941).

Murray, Andrew, *Holiest of All* (Westwood, NJ: Revell Publishers, 1960).

Nouwen, Henri J.M., quotation from Nouwen's *A Cry for Mercy* in Job and Shawchuck, *A Guide to Prayer* (Nashville: The Upper Room, 1983).

Ortlund, Raymond C., *Lord, Make My Life a Miracle* (Ventura, CA: Regal Press, 1974).

Owen, John, *Communion with God*, abridged and made easy to read by R.J.K. Law (Edinborough, Scotland, and Carlisle, PA: the Banner of Truth Trust, 1991).

Peterson, Eugene, "Spirit Quest," in *Christianity Today*, Nov. 8, 1993.

Tozer, A.W., *The Knowledge of the Holy* (New York: Harper and Row, 1961).

Wood, A. Skevington, quotation from Skevington's *Evangelism: Its Theology and Practice,* in *Christianity Today,* Nov. 8, 1993.